Ghosts in Solid Form

By Gambier Bolton

Copyright © 2020 Lamp of Trismegistus. All rights reserved. No part of this publication may be reproduced or transmitted in any form or by any means, electronic or mechanical, including photocopying, recording, or by any information storage and retrieval system, without permission in writing from Lamp of Trismegistus. Reviewers may quote brief passages.

ISBN: 978-1-63118-469-7

*Paranormal Research
Series*

Other Books in this Series and Related Titles

The Tree of Wisdom by Nagarjuna (978-1-63118-470-3)

Fortune-Telling with Dice by Astra Cielo (978-1-63118-466-6)

American Indian Freemasonry by A. C. Parker (978-1-63118-460-4)

The Rosicrucian Chemical Marriage by Christian Rosenkreuz (978-1-63118-458-1)

The Gospel of the Nativity of Mary by St. Matthew (978-1-63118-448-2)

Ancient Mysteries & Secret Societies by M. P. Hall (978-1-63118-410-9)

Arcane Formulas or Mental Alchemy by W. W. Atkinson (978-1-63118-459-8)

Magical Essays and Instructions by Florence Farr (978-1-63118-418-5)

Alchemy in the Nineteenth Century by H. P. Blavatsky (978-1-63118-446-8)

Crystal Vision Through Crystal Gazing by Achad (978-1-63118-455-0)

Dreams and Their Interpretation by Astra Cielo (978-1-63118-468-0)

The Machinery of the Mind by Dion Fortune (978-1-63118-451-2)

The Secrets of Enoch by Enoch (978-1-63118-449-9)

Fortune-Telling by Playing Cards by Astra Cielo (978-1-63118-467-3)

The Old Past Master by Carl H. Claudy (978-1-63118-464-2)

The Path of Light: A Manual of Maha-Yana Buddhism by Barnett (978-1-63118-471-0)

Buddhist Psalms by Shinran (978-1-63118-465-9)

Psalms of Solomon by King Solomon (978-1-63118-439-0)

An Outline of Theosophy by C. W. Leadbeater (978-1-63118-452-9)

Thirty-One Hymns to the Star Goddess by Achad (978-1-63118-422-2)

Cloud Upon the Sanctuary by K. Eckartshausen (978-1-63118-438-3)

Audio Versions are also Available on Audible and iTunes

Table of Contents

Foreword...7

Chapter 1
Conditions...9

Chapter 2
Precautions Against Fraud...19

Chapter 3
Tests...33

Chapter 4
Questions Answered By Various Entities...59

Appendix...93

FOREWORD

As scientists in many parts of the world today are turning their serious attention to the question of the origin and the (possible) continuity of Life, I feel that the time has now arrived when a text-book on the subject of the phenomena, known to investigators as Materializations, should be issued to the public, in order to assist inquirers, both scientists and laymen, in their endeavor to solve these vitally important matters; as, in my opinion, it is by no means improbable that in Materializations we may find the clue which will eventually enable us to solve the question, asked by each cradle, "Whence?" and by each coffin, "Whither?"

This text-book contains, in plain and simple language the results of a series of experiments carried out during a period of seven years. With the exception of a few conducted by that master scientist Sir William Crookes, President of the Royal Society, London, and referred to in Chapter III. (to which mine were in the nature of a sequel), all were carried out in my presence; and the reports on these experiments have been collated from the official records kept by my three research societies in London.

CHAPTER 1
CONDITIONS

"A single grain of solid fact is worth ten tons of theory."

"The more I think of it, the more I find this conclusion impressed upon me, that the greatest thing a human soul ever does in this world is to SEE something and tell what it saw in a plain way. Hundreds of people can talk for one who can think, but thousands can think for one who can see. To SEE clearly is poetry, prophecy and religion all in one."—JOHN RUSKIN.

WORKING HYPOTHESIS

That under certain known and reasonable conditions of temperature, light, etc., entities, existing In a sphere outside our own, have been demonstrated again and again to manifest themselves on earth in temporary bodies materialized from an, at present, undiscovered source, through the agency of certain persons of both sexes, termed Sensitives, and can be so demonstrated to any person who will provide the conditions proved to be necessary for such a demonstration.

Looking back to the seven years of my life which I devoted to a careful and critical investigation of the claim made, not only by both Occidental and Oriental mystics, but by well-known men of science like Sir William Crookes, Professor Alfred Russel Wallace, and others—that it was possible under certain clearly defined conditions to produce, apparently out of nothing, fully formed bodies, inhabited by (presumably) human entities from another sphere—the wonder of it still enthralls me; the apparent impossibility of so great an upheaval of such laws of Nature as we are at present acquainted with, being proved clearly to be possible, will remain to the end as "the wonder of wonders" in a by no means uneventful life.

For, as compared with this, that greatest of Nature's mysteries, the procreation of a human infant—by either the normal or mechanical impregnation of an ovum—its months of fetal growth and development in the uterus, and its birth into the world in a helpless and enfeebled condition, amazing as they are to all physiological students,—sinks into comparative insignificance when compared with the nearly instantaneous production of a fully developed human body, with all its organs functioning properly; a body inhabited temporarily by a thinking, reasoning entity, who can see, hear, taste, smell and touch: a body which can be handled, weighed, measured, and photographed.

When these claims were first brought to my notice I realized at once that I was face to face with a problem which would require the very closest investigation; and I then and there decided to give up work of all kinds, and to devote years, if necessary, to a critical examination of these claims; to investigate the matter calmly and dispassionately, and, in Sir John Herschel's memorable words, "to stand or fall by the result of a direct appeal to facts in the first instance, and of strict logical deduction from them afterwards."

And, as I have said, the result has been that the apparently impossible has been proved to be possible; and I accept them wholeheartedly, admitting that our working hypothesis has been proved beyond any possibility of doubt, and that these materialized entities can manifest themselves today to any person who will provide the conditions necessary for such a demonstration.

Who they are, what they are, whence they come, and whither they go, each investigator must determine for himself; but of their actual existence in a sphere just outside our own, there can no longer be any room for doubt. As a busy man, theories have little or no attraction for me. What I demand, and what other busy men and women demand, in an investigation of this kind is, that there should be a reasonable possibility of getting hold of facts, good solid facts which can be demonstrated as such, to any open-minded inquirer, otherwise it would be useless to commence such an investigation. And we have now got these facts, and can prove them on purely scientific lines.

The meaning of the word Materialization, so far at least as it concerns our investigation, I understand to be this: the taking on by an entity from a sphere outside our own, an entity representing a man, woman, or child (or even a beast or bird), of a temporary body built up from material drawn partially from the inhabitants of earth, consolidated through the agency of certain persons of both sexes, termed Sensitives, and molded by the entity into a semblance of the body which (it alleges) it inhabited during its existence on earth. In other words, a materialization is the appearance of an entity in bodily, tangible form (i.e. one which we can touch), thus differing from an astralization, etherealization, or apparition, which is, of course, one which cannot be touched, although it may be clearly visible to anyone possessing only normal sight.

Let me, then, endeavor to describe to the best of my ability, and in very simple language, how I believe these materializations to be produced, and the conditions which I have proved to be necessary in order that the finest results may be obtained.

I will deal first with the question of as without conditions of some kind no materialization can be produced, any more than a scientific experiment—such as mixing various chemicals together, in order to produce a certain result—can be carried out successfully without proper conditions being provided by the experimenter. What, then, do we mean by this word "conditions"?

Take a homely example. The baker mixes exactly the right quantities of flour, salt, and yeast with water, and then places the "dough" which he has made in an oven heated to just the right temperature, and produces a loaf of bread. Why? Because the conditions were good ones. Had he omitted the flour, the yeast, or the water, or had he used an oven over or under heated, he could not have produced an eatable loaf of bread, because the conditions made it impossible.

This is what is meant by the terms, "Good conditions," "Bad conditions," "Breaking conditions."

The conditions, then, under which I have been able to prove to many hundreds of inquirers that it is possible for materialized entities to appear on earth, in solid tangible form, are these :

First, Light of suitable wave-length (i.e. suitable color), and let me say here, once and for all, that I have proved conclusively for myself that provided that one is experimenting with a Sensitive who has been trained to sit always in the light.

On two occasions I have witnessed materializations in daylight; and neither of Sir William Crookes' Sensitives—D. P. Home or Florrie Cook (Mrs. Corner)—would ever sit in darkness: the latter, with whom I carried out a long series of experiments, invariably stipulating that a good light should be used during the whole time that the experiment lasted, as she was terrified at the mere thought of darkness.

I find that sunlight, electric light, gas, colza oil, and paraffin are all apt to check the production of the phenomena unless filtered through canary-yellow, orange, or red linen or paper—just as they are filtered for photographic purposes—owing to the violent action of the actinic (blue) rays which they contain (the rays from the violet end of the spectrum), which are said to work at about six hundred billions of vibrations per second. But if the light is filtered, in the way that I have described, the production of the phenomena will commence at once, the vibrations of the Interfering rays being reduced; it is said, to about four hundred billions per second or less.

In dealing with materializations we are apt to overlook the fact that we are investigating forces or modes of energy far more delicate than electricity, for instance. Heat, electricity, and light, as Sir William Crookes tells us are all closely related: we know the awful power of heat and electricity, but are only too apt to forget—especially if it suits our purpose to do so—that light too has enormous dynamic potency; its vibrations being said to travel In space at the incredible speed of twelve million miles a minute; and it is therefore only reasonable to assume that the power of these vibrations may be sufficient to interfere seriously with the more subtle forces, such as those which we are now investigating.

Secondly, we require suitable heat vibrations, and I find that those given off in a room either warmed or chilled to sixty-three degrees are the very best possible; anything either much above this, or, more especially, much below this, tending to weaken the results and to check the phenomena.

Thirdly, we require suitable musical vibrations, and, after carrying out a long series of experiments with musical instruments of all kinds, I find that the vibrations given off by the reed organ—termed "harmonium" or "American organ,"—or by the concertina, are the most suitable, the peculiar quality of the vibrations given off by the reeds in these instruments proving to be the most suitable ones for use during the production of the phenomena; although on one or two occasions I have obtained good results without musical vibrations of any kind, but this is rare.

Fourthly, we require the presence of a specially organized man or woman, termed one from whom it is alleged a portion of the matter used by the entity in the building up of its temporary body can be drawn, with but little chance of injury to their health. This point is one of vital importance, we are told, for it has been proved by means of a self-registering weighing-machine on which he was seated, and to which he was securely fastened with an electrical apparatus secretly hidden beneath the seat, which would at once ring a bell in an anteroom if he endeavored to rise from his seat during the experiment, that the actual loss in weight to the Sensitive, when a fully materialized entity was standing in our midst, was no less than sixty-five pounds!

Before employing any person, then, as a Sensitive for these delicate, not to say dangerous, experiments, he or she should be medically examined, in the interests of both the investigator and the Sensitive, and should their health prove to be in any way below par, they should not be permitted to take part in the experiment until their health is fully restored.

I have been permitted to examine the Sensitive at the moment when an entity, clad in a fully-formed temporary body, was walking amongst the experimenters; and the distorted features, the shriveled-up limbs and contorted trunk of the Sensitive at that moment proclaimed the danger connected with the production of this special form of phenomena far louder than any words of mine could do.

Needless to say, Sensitives for materializations are extremely rare, not more than two or three being found today amidst the teeming millions who inhabit the British Islands; although a few are to be found on the European continent, and several in North America, where the climatic conditions are said to be more favorable for the development of such persons.

Now, what constitutes a Sensitive, and why are they necessary?

Sensitives through whom physical phenomena (including materializations) can be produced have been described, firstly, as persons in whom certain forces are stored up, either far in excess of the amount possessed by the normal man or woman, or else differing in quality from the forces stored up by the normal man or woman; and secondly, as persons who are able to attract from those in close proximity to them—provided that the conditions are favorable—still more of the force, which thus becomes centered in them for the time being. In other words, a Sensitive for physical phenomena is said to be for the force which is used in the production of physical phenomena—including materializations—although it is by no means improbable that such highly developed Sensitives as those required for this special purpose may be found to possess extra nerve-centers as compared with those possessed by normal human beings. But whether this hypothesis be eventually proved or not, there seems to be but very little doubt that "whatever the force may be which constitutes the difference between a Sensitive and a non-Sensitive, it is certainly of a mental or magnetic character, i.e. a combination of the subtle elements of mind and magnetism, and therefore of a psychological, and not of a purely physical character."

But why is a Sensitive necessary? you ask. Think of a telephone for a moment. You wish to communicate with a person who is holding only the end of the wire in his hand, the result being that he cannot hear a single word.

Why is this? Because he has forgotten to fit a "receiver" at his end of the wire, a "receiver" in which the vibrations set up by your voice may be centralized, focused; a "receiver" which he can place to his ear, and in doing so will at once hear your voice distinctly; but without this your message to him is lost.

And it is said that this is exactly the use of the Sensitives during our experiments, for they act as "receivers" in which the forces employed in the production of the phenomena may be centralized, focused: their varying degrees of sensitiveness enabling them to be used by the entities in other spheres for the successful production of such phenomena, we are told.

And lastly, we require about twelve to sixteen earnest and really sympathetic men and women—persons trained on scientific lines for choice—all in the best of health: men and women who, whilst strictly on their guard against anything in the shape of fraud, are still so much in sympathy with the person who is acting as the Sensitive that they are all the time sending out kindly thoughts towards him; for if, as has been said, "thoughts are things," it is possible that hostile thoughts would be sufficient not only to enfeeble, but actually to check demonstrations of physical phenomena of all kinds in the presence of such specially organized, highly developed individuals as the Sensitives through whom materializations can be produced.

I shall refer to these men and women as THE SITTERS.

We generally select an equal number so far as sex is concerned; and in addition, we endeavor to obtain an equal number of persons possessing either positive or negative temperaments. In this way we form the Sitters into a powerful human battery, the combined force given off by them (if the battery is properly arranged, and the individual members of that battery are in good health) proving of enormous assistance during our experiments. If in ill-health, we find that a man or woman is useless to us: for we can no more expect to obtain the necessary power from such an individual, than we can expect to produce an electric spark from a discharged accumulator, or pick up needles with a demagnetized piece of steel.

We are told to remember always that "all manifestations of natural laws are the results of natural conditions."

Minor details too, we find, must be thought out most carefully if we are to provide what we may term ideal conditions.

The chairs should be made of wood throughout; those known as Austrian bentwood chairs, having perforated seats, being proved to be the best for the purpose.

The Sitters should bathe and then change their clothing—the ladies into white dresses, and the men into dark suits—two hours before the time fixed for the experiment, and should then at once partake of a light meal—meat and alcohol being strictly forbidden—so that the strain upon their constitutions during the experiment may not interfere with their health.

Trivial as such matters must appear to the man in the street, we are told they must all be carried out most carefully, in order that the finest conditions possible may be obtained; the one great object of the Sitters being to give off all the power—and the best kind of power—that they are capable of producing, in order that sufficient suitable material may be gathered together from the Sensitive and themselves, with which a temporary body may be formed for the use of any entity wishing to materialize in their presence.

CHAPTER 2
PRECAUTIONS AGAINST FRAUD

"Nothing is too wonderful to be true."—FARADAY.

We are now ready to see what happens at a typical experimental meeting for these materializations, at hundreds of which I have assisted, and having the services of no less than six Sensitives placed at my disposal for purpose. I will endeavor to describe it; I should consider to be an ideal one, held under ideal (test) conditions.

Our imaginary test meeting is to be carried out—as it was on one occasion in London—In an entirely empty house, which none of us have ever entered before, a house which we will hire for this special event. By doing this we may feel sure that all possibility of fraud, so tar as the use of secret trap-doors, large mirrors, and other undesirable things of that description are concerned, can be successfully thwarted.

I would ask you to bear in mind that we are about to take part in A PURELY SCIENTIFIC EXPERIMENT; and, whether I weary you with my descriptions or not, I intend to take just as elaborate precautions against trickery, so far as the room in which this imaginary meeting is to take place is concerned, as if I were at work getting a room ready for an actual test meeting; for I intend to leave no possible loop-hole for fraud, otherwise our time will be wasted.

And I am going to take equally elaborate precautions to prevent trickery on the part of those attending this meeting, either as Sitters or Sensitive, treating one and all alike, however harsh this treatment may seem to be. But in a matter of such gravity I can trust no one, but must assume that every person attending the meeting is capable of assisting in the production of fraudulent phenomena—Sitters and Sensitive alike—and I shall take such preliminary precautions as will render trickery absolutely impossible by anyone present at this imaginary meeting.

Harsh as it may seem, it is the only possible attitude for an open-minded investigator to assume in a matter of such vital importance as this; one which strikes down to the very roots of our existence as human beings, the origin and the—possible—continuity of life; to the very roots of our social and legal systems; to the very roots of our various religions. For we must bear in mind that, during this experiment, we are to deal with a certain alleged fact, the possibility of entities from another sphere returning to earth in visible, tangible bodies; reasoning, thinking entities who are able to tell us of their life in other spheres; who proclaim the falsity of much that we regard as sacred—and we must therefore demand the most stringent tests that human ingenuity can devise, in order that we may be able to prove the truth or the falsity of the alleged fact. No other course is possible, in my opinion, for the investigator who is entering for the first time upon this little-known field of research.

Such vast numbers of persons, such incredible numbers, attended the experimental meetings which I instituted in London for the examination of this alleged fact—persons from all parts of Great Britain; all parts of Europe, Canada, and the Americas; from far-off Japan, China, Burmah, India, Africa, Australia, and other portions of the world; persons in all stations of life, from those closely and intimately connected with the royal family; members of the royal household; distinguished soldiers like Field-Marshal Lord Wolseley, General Carrington, General Sir Alfred Turner, General Gordon and Colonel Valentine Gordon—both relatives of the great General Gordon—and numerous other officers of the highest rank; distinguished sailors like my friend Vice-Admiral Usborne Moore—a painstaking and highly critical investigator, who witnessed his first materializations at these meetings; great physicians from Harley Street, London, and elsewhere, including the distinguished head of the Army Medical Department, Surgeon-General Fawcett; members of the diplomatic services from nearly every civilized nation on earth; officials from the Treasury, the Foreign Office, the India Office, the Colonial Office, and the War Office; members of the House of Lords, members of the House of Commons—of all the many known shades of political opinion; great journalists like W. T. Stead, and many others from different parts of the world; great writers like Sir Arthur Conan Doyle, John Oliver Hobbes (Mrs Craigie), Florence Marryat, and many others; great scientists like Signor Marconi; celebrated ecclesiastics of almost every degree, and holding innumerable creeds and dogmas (some of them carefully disguised as laymen, and passing under assumed names); well-known actors and actresses; well-known musicians, singers, artists, and architects; men and women of all kinds, each in his or her own way what the world terms "celebrities," with many hundreds of others who make no claim to that title—such an incredible number of persons attended our experimental meetings in London that it is quite possible that out of that vast number you yourself may have attended one or more of them, and may be thinking that at the meetings to which you were admitted the conditions were not nearly so elaborately thought out, the tests were not nearly so stringent, as those which I am about to impose upon the Sitters and the Sensitive at the imaginary one in which we are now about to take part.

That is quite possible; for at the ordinary experimental meetings held by my three societies, the conditions imposed were widely different to those insisted upon at our test meetings—such as those held with Florrie Cook (Mrs. Corner), which were strictly confined not only to members, but to specially selected members.

I would ask you to remember too that I am not describing the conditions imposed or the results obtained at any particular meeting at which I was present; but rather the conditions which I consider should be provided, and the precautions against trickery which I consider ought to be taken in a really scientifically carried out experiment for materializations.

Having all met together at an appointed hour in the hail of the empty house which we have hired for the night—all, that is, with the exception of the Sensitive, who is not permitted to enter the house until half an hour later—it is put to the vote as to which room shall be used for this meeting; and as soon as that is settled, we all walk up to, and into, it together, and find ourselves in a large and lofty room on the second floor absolutely empty.

Looking out of the window we see that there is a sheer drop of (say) fifty feet to the street below, and, as there are no houses anywhere in its immediate proximity, we are satisfied that it is altogether impossible for any person to either enter or leave the room by the window.

Turning our attention to the room itself, we see that there are four bare walls, with a gas-bracket fitted into one of them, a ceiling, a fireplace, and a solid floor. These must be critically examined first by an expert, and next the means of entrance to and exit from the room—the door, window, and fireplace.

I have purposely included amongst the Sitters a well-known London doctor, an equally well-known London architect—both extremely skeptical, as they actually were at one time, as to the possibility of obtaining results unless fraud was introduced—and also two persons who have developed to a high degree their powers of second-sight (clairvoyance or clear-seeing), and shall make great use of them all during the meeting, as I frequently did when experimenting in London.

We hand the key of the room to you, and all, with the exception of the architect and yourself, then leave the room, it being your duty to watch the architect carefully whilst he carries out a critical professional examination of the empty room. He will then draw up a report, which you will both sign, saying that in your opinion the room is not "prepared" in any way, but is in a perfectly normal state.

You then unlock the door and hand out the signed report; and we at once pass in to you seventeen chairs, a large photographic lamp (with a piece of India-rubber tubing, for you to attach from the lamp to the gas-bracket as fitted in the wall of the room), a strong wooden cover which fits tightly into the fireplace (with long screws and a screwdriver to enable you to fasten it securely in position), a piece of dark-colored cloth or baize for you to nail up over the window (with a hammer and nails) so as to exclude all actinic light, and we push in a small harmonium and a music-stool.

Directly these are handed to you, you lock the door, and the architect joins with you in a close examination of each article; and when you are both satisfied that none of the articles are "prepared" in any way, you draw up a second report, which you both sign, stating that nothing whatever is, or can possibly be, concealed in them. You then both come out of the room, locking the door behind you and keeping the key in your possession.

Having thus dealt with the room, and every article inside the room in which our experiment is to be conducted, we now proceed to deal with each person who intends to be present during the experiment—the doctor, the architect, you yourself, and I myself, with the remainder of the Sitters, men and women alike, one and all being treated in exactly the same way, however harsh it may seem, for in a matter of such importance as this we can trust no one.

The doctor takes each Sitter alone into an adjoining room. Every article of clothing is removed in each case and the doctor then makes a careful examination to see that the person has nothing in his or her possession concealed about their bodies, or in their clothing, which could be used in assisting to produce fraudulent phenomena. At the conclusion of this searching examination, the Sitter is permitted to dress, and you then show him (or her) into the empty room, you yourself unlocking the door to admit them and locking it after them.

The Sensitive now arrives at the house, and is met by the doctor, who takes him into the adjoining room and at once carries out a searching examination of the Sensitive's body. His clothes are taken away from him, and, at the conclusion of the search, he is lent a complete outfit for the evening, in case he should have secret pockets in his own clothing. If the Sensitive is a woman she is treated in exactly the same way; and, after her clothing has been taken away from her, she is lent, not only a black dress, but a complete set of black underclothing for use during the experiment, even her white pocket-handkerchief being taken from her before she enters the room, so that she cannot possibly masquerade as an entity clad in white draperies.

When the search is over, and the change of clothing has been completed, you unlock the door, and the Sensitive is admitted to the room for the first time.

All are now in the room with the exception of the doctor; and it is then put to the vote as to who shall pass out and carefully examine the doctor, and only this Sitter is permitted to go out of the room. On the completion of the examination, the doctor and the Sitter return to the room, and the door is finally locked and bolted, you retaining the key during the whole evening.

The large gas-lamp on the mantelpiece has of course been lit previous to this, and the flame is now turned up fully. The Sensitive takes his seat on a chair placed in a corner of the room furthest away from the door, the window, and the fireplace; the Sitters placing their sixteen chairs in a half-circle round him, so that he can only escape from his chair into the room by climbing over the Sitters.

The architect is then given strips of gummed paper and a stylographic pen. He and you paste these strips round the door, the window, and the fireplace, writing on the strips of paper any word or words selected by yourselves and known only to you, so that, in the event of their being tampered with, you would be able to see at once that the paper had been broken.

One of the Sitters, who is a musician, takes his seat temporarily at the harmonium, and commences to play suitable music, and we are ready to start our experiment; the general feeling of all those in the room being that every possible precaution against trickery has been taken, and that if any results of any kind whatever should follow they will undoubtedly be genuine.

The Sitters having been allotted their seats, so that a person of a positive and a person of a negative temperament shall be seated together, we now join hands, and form ourselves into what we are told is a powerful human battery; the two persons sitting at the two ends of the half-circle having of course each one hand free: and from the free hands of these two persons, it is said, the power developed and given off by this human battery passes into the Sensitive at each of his sides.

Sitting quietly in our chairs and talking gently amongst ourselves, we soon feel a cool breeze blowing across our hands. In another two minutes this will have so increased in volume that it may with truth be described as a strong wind.

On looking at the Sensitive now, we see that he is rapidly passing into a state of trance—his head is drooping on one side, his arms and hands hang downwards loosely, his body being in a limp real trance condition, and just in the right state for use by any entity desiring to work through him, we are told.

I have only experimented with one Sensitive who did not pass into trance, but, seated amongst the Sitters, he remained in a perfectly normal condition during the whole of the experiment; watching the materialized forms building up beside him, and talking to and with them during the process. I shall refer to him shortly.

We now set our clairvoyants to work, and the statements made by one must be confirmed in every detail by the statements of the other as to what is occurring at the moment, or no notice is taken of their remarks.

Both now report that they see a thin white mist or 'vapor' coming from the left side of the Sensitive, if a man (or from the pelvis, if a woman), which passes into the Sitter at the end of the half-circle nearest to the Sensitive's left side. It then passes, they state, from Sitter No. 1 to Sitter No. 2, and so on, until it has gone through the whole of the sixteen Sitters, passing finally from the last one (No. 16) at the end of the half-circle nearest to the Sensitive's right side, and disappears into his right side.

We assume from this that the nerve force, magnetic power—call it what YOU will—necessary for the formation of one of these temporary bodies starts from the Sensitive, passes through each Sitter, drawing from each as much more force or power as he or she is capable of giving off at the moment, returning to the Sensitive greatly increased in its amount and ready for use in the next process. This, then, we will term the first of the three stages in the evolution of an entity clad in a temporary body:

THE VAPOR STAGE

In a few moments our clairvoyants both report that the force or power is issuing from the side of the Sensitive, if a man (or from the pelvis, if a woman), in the form of a white, soft, dough-like substance,' which on one occasion I was permitted to touch. I could perceive no smell given off by it; it felt cold and clammy, and appeared to have the consistency of heavy dough at the moment that I touched it.

This mass of dough-like substance is said to be the material used by the entities—one by one as a rule—who wish to build up a temporary body. It seems to rest on the floor, somewhere near the right side of the Sensitive, until required for use: its bulk depending apparently upon the amount of power given off by the Sitters from time to time during the experiment.

This we will term the second of the three stages of the evolution of an entity clad in a temporary body:

THE SOLID, BUT SHAPELESS STAGE

We are told that the entity wishing to show himself to us passes into this shapeless mass of dough-like substance, which at once increases in bulk, and commences to pulsate and move up and down, swaying from side to side as it grows in height, the motive power being evidently underneath.

The entity then quickly sets to work to mold the mass into something resembling a human body, commencing with the head. The rest of the upper portion of the body soon follows, and the heart and pulse can now be felt to be beating quite regularly and normally, differing in this respect from those of the Sensitive, who, if tested at this time, will be found with both heart and pulse-beats considerably above the normal. The legs and feet come last, and then the entity is able to leave the near neighborhood of the Sensitive and to walk amongst the Sitters, THE THIRD AND LAST STAGE of its evolution being now complete.

Although occasionally the entity will appear clad in an exact copy of the clothing which he states that he wore when on earth—

especially if it should happen to be something a little out of the common, such as a military or naval uniform—they are draped as a rule in flowing white garments of a wonderfully soft texture, and this too I have been permitted to handle.

Our clairvoyants both affirm that at all times during the materialization a thin band of, presumably, the dough-like substance can be plainly seen issuing from the side of the Sensitive, if a man (or from the pelvis, if a woman), and joined on to the center of the body inhabited by the entity—just like the umbilical cord attached to a human infant at birth,—and we are instructed that this band cannot be stretched beyond a certain radius, say ten to fifteen feet, without doing harm to the Sensitive and to the entity: although cases are on record where materializations have been seen at a distance of nearly sixty feet from the Sensitive, on occasions when the conditions were unusually favorable.

On handling different portions of the materialized body now, the flesh is found to be both warm and firm. The bodies are well proportioned, those of the females—for they take on sex conditions during the process—having beautiful figures; and hands, arms, legs, and feet quite perfect in their modeling: but, in my opinion, the body, head, and limbs of every materialization of either sex or any age which I have scrutinized at close quarters carefully, or have been permitted to handle, have appeared to be at least one-third smaller in size (except as regards actual height) than those possessed by beings on earth of the same sex and age.

Not only have we witnessed materializations of aged entities of both sexes, showing all the characteristics of old age, for the purpose of identification by the Sitters, as they tell us—but we have seen materialized infants also; and on one occasion two still-born children appeared in our midst simultaneously, one of them showing distinct traces on its little face of a hideous deformity which it possessed at the time of his premature birth—a deformity known only to the mother, who happened to be present that evening as one of the Sitters.

We are told that, for the purpose of identification, the entity will return to earth in an exact counterpart of the body which he alleges that he occupied at the time of his death, and in order that he may be recognized by his relatives and friends who happen to be present. Thus, the one who left the earth as an infant will appear in his materialized body as an infant, although he may have been dead for twenty or thirty years. The aged man or woman will appear with bent body, wrinkled face, and snow-white hair, walking amongst us with difficulty, and just as they allege they did before their death, although that may have occurred twenty years before. The one who had lose a limb during his earth-life will return minus that limb; the one who was disfigured by accident or disease will return bearing distinct traces of that disfigurement, for the purpose of identification only.

But as soon as the identification has been established successfully, all this changes instantly: the disfigurement disappears: the four limbs will be seen, and both the infant and the aged will from henceforth show themselves to us in the very prime of life—the young growing upwards and the aged downwards, as we say, and, as they one and all state emphatically, just as they really look and feel in the sphere in which they now exist.

While inhabiting these temporary bodies, they state that they take on, not only sex conditions, but earth conditions temporarily too: for they appear to feel pain if their bodies are injured m any way; complain of the cold if the temperature of the room is allowed to fail much below sixty degrees, or of the heat if the temperature is allowed to rise above seventy degrees; seem to be depressed during a thunderstorm, when our atmosphere is overcharged with electricity; and appear bright and happy in a warm room when the world outside is in the grip of a hard frost, and also on bright, starry nights.

And not only this, but they take on strongly marked characteristics of the numerous races on earth temporarily too: the materialized entities of the white races differing quite as markedly from those of the yellow or brown races, as do these from the black races; and in speaking to us each one will communicate in the particular language only which is characteristic of his race on earth.

Five, six, and even seven totally different languages have been employed during a single experimental meeting through a Sensitive who had never in his life been out of England, and who was proved conclusively to know no other language than English: the latter number, we were told, being in honor of a ship's doctor who was present on one occasion, and who—although the fact was quite unknown to any of us at the time—proved to be an expert linguist, for he conversed that evening with different entities in English, French, German, Russian, Chinese, Japanese, and in the language of one of the hill-tribes of India.

On another occasion, when I was the only European present at an afternoon experimental meeting held in London by eight Parsees of both sexes from Bombay, during the whole of the time—two and a quarter hours—which the meeting lasted the entities and the Parsee Sitters carried on their conversation in Hindustani; two entities simultaneously and one of the Parsee men engaging in a heated controversy, which lasted for nearly three minutes, over the disposal of the bodies of their dead: the entities insisting on cremation only, as opposed to allowing the bodies to be eaten by vultures—the noise which they made during this discussion being almost deafening. The Sensitive, it was proved conclusively, knew no other language than English, and had only once been out of the British Islands, when he paid a short visit to France.

CHAPTER 3
TESTS

"Sit down before a fact as a little child: be prepared to give up every preconceived notion: follow humbly wherever and to whatever abysses Nature leads, or you shall learn nothing."
—THOMAS HUXLEY

The tests given to me and to my fellow investigators through the six Sensitives who so ably assisted us during our seven years of experimental work in this little-known field of research—the tests have been so numerous, and were of such a varied character, that I find it somewhat difficult to know which to select out of the hundreds which were recorded in our books officially and elsewhere, the ones which will prove of the greatest interest to inquirers; but I have made extracts from ten of these records, and these, with a few taken from Sir William Crookes' reports on the experiments conducted in his presence, will, in my opinion, be sufficient to prove that we who have witnessed these marvels are neither hallucinated, insane, nor liars when we solemnly affirm that we have both seen and handled the materialized bodies built up for temporary use by entities from another sphere: all the statements made here being true in every detail, to the best of my knowledge and belief.

EXPERIMENT No. 1

Place—Lyndhurst, New Forest, Hampshire. Sensitive A, male, aged about 46.

As an example of a simple but exceedingly severe test, I would first record one given to me and a fellow-investigator on the outskirts of the New Forest; one for which no special preparation of any kind whatever had been made.

The Sensitive, a nearly blind man, was taken by us on a dark night to a spot totally unknown to him, as he had only just arrived from London by train, and was led into a large traveling caravan, one which he had never been near before, as it had only recently left the builder's hands.

During the day I had made a critical examination of the interior of the caravan, and had satisfied myself that no one was or could possibly be concealed in it. I then locked the door, and kept the key in my pocket until the moment when, on the arrival of the Sensitive, I unlocked the door and we all passed into the caravan together. I then locked and bolted the door behind us.

As I have already said, no preparation of any kind had been made for the experiment. It was merely the result of a desire to see if anything could be produced, through this Sensitive, under extremely difficult conditions—conditions which we considered as so utterly bad as to make failure a certainty.

We did not even possess a chair of any kind for the Sensitive or ourselves to sit upon, so we placed for his use a board on top of the iron cooking-range which was fixed in the kitchen portion of the caravan, whilst we sat upon the two couches which were used as beds in the living-portion of the caravan. There was no music, no powerful "human battery" in the shape of a number of picked Sitters; in fact, the conditions were just about as bad as they could possibly be, and yet, within ten minutes of my locking the door behind us, the figure of a tall man stood before us, a man so tall that he was compelled to bow his head as he passed under the six-foot (high) partition which separated the two sections of the caravan.

He said, "I am Colonel__ who was 'killed', as you say, at the battle of __ in Egypt. For many years during my earth-life I was deeply interested in materializations, and spent the last night of my life in England experimenting with this very Sensitive; and it is a great pleasure to me to be able to return to you—strangers though you both are to me—through him. To prove to you that I am not the Sensitive masquerading before you, will you please come here and stand close to me, and so settle the matter for yourself?"

I at once rose and stood beside him, almost touching him. I then discovered that not only were his features and his coloring totally different to those of the Sensitive, but that he towered above me, standing, as nearly as I could judge, six foot two or three inches, and was certainly four inches taller than either the Sensitive or myself.

Whilst thus standing beside him, and at a distance of about eight feet from the Sensitive, we could both hear the unfortunate man moving uneasily on his hard seat on the kitchen-range, sighing and moaning as if in pain.

The entity remained with us for about three minutes, and his place was then taken by a slightly built young man, standing about five feet nine inches, one claiming to be a recently deceased member of the royal family. He talked with us in a soft and pleasing voice, finally whispering a private message to my companion, asking him to deliver it to his mother, Queen.

EXPERIMENT No. 2

Place—Peckham Rye, London, S.E. Sensitive A, male, aged about 46.

An almost equally hopeless task was set this Sensitive by the owner of the caravan and myself when we experimented with him at midday on a brilliant morning in July, with sunlight streaming into the room round the edges of the drawn down window-blinds, and round the top, sides, and bottom of the heavy window-curtains, which we had pinned together in a vain attempt to keep out the sunlight during the experiment.

And yet, once again, and in spite of the conditions which we regarded as utterly hopeless, the figure of a man appeared in less than ten minutes, materialized from head to foot, as he proved to us by showing us his lower limbs. He left the side of the Sensitive, walked out into the room and stood between us, talking to us in a deep rich voice for nearly three minutes. As he stood beside us we could hear the Sensitive, twelve feet away, moving uneasily on his chair and groaning slightly.

Five minutes after he disappeared the same (alleged) recently deceased member of the royal family walked out to us and held a short private conversation with my companion, and sent another message to his mother, Queen.

EXPERIMENT No. 3

Place—West Hampstead, London, N.W. Sensitive B, female, aged about 49.

Persons of middle age or older who happened to be in England a few years ago at the time that two lawsuits were brought against a celebrated conjurer by the clever young man who had succeeded in exposing one of his most mystifying tricks, will well remember the sensation caused by the giving of both verdicts against the conjurer; and the young man—to whom I shall refer—as Mr. X.—at once became famous as the man who had beaten one of the cleverest conjurers of the day.

A friend of mine, who had been present on several occasions when Sir William Crookes' Sensitive—Florrie Cook (Mrs. Corner), referred to above as Sensitive B—had produced materializations in gaslight at my house in London, asked her to visit his house at West Hampstead one evening to meet several friends of his, and to see if it were possible for any entity to materialize in my friend's own drawing-room.

She at once accepted his invitation to sit there under strict test conditions; and talking the matter over with some of his friends a day or two before the one chosen for the experiment, he told me that they had arranged to have the Sensitive securely tied to her chair, to have strong iron rings fastened to the floor-boards, through which ropes would be passed, these ropes to be securely fastened to the Sensitive's legs; all knots of every size and kind to be sealed, so as to prevent any attempt on her part to leave her chair and to masquerade as a materialized entity.

One of his friends happened to know the celebrated Mr. X., and as he had so recently succeeded in beating so notable a conjurer, he was invited to be present and to take entire charge of the tying up, the binding and sealing arrangements, in order to render the escape of the Sensitive from her chair an impossibility.

When I joined the party in the drawing-room, Mr. X., to whom I was introduced, was busily engaged in tying the Sensitive up with his own ropes and tapes, sealing every knot with special sealing-wax and with a seal provided by our host. The room was a large one, and a portion at one end had been cleared of all furniture, and in the center of this space only the Sensitive seated upon her chair, and Mr. X. busily at work, were to be seen; and the latter, after another fifteen minutes of real hard labor, was asked by our host if he was thoroughly satisfied that the Sensitive was fastened to her chair securely. He replied that so securely was she fastened, that if she could produce phenomena of any kind whatever under such conditions, he would at once admit their genuineness.

The Sensitive was all this time in a perfectly normal state, and not flurried in any way, her one anxiety being lest we should lower the lights, as she was so terrified at the thought of darkness.

Mr. X., after stepping backwards to have a final look at the result of his labors, then walked close to the spot where the Sensitive was sitting in gaslight, and put one hand up towards the top of the curtain, and was in the act of drawing this round her to keep the direct rays of the gaslight from falling upon her, when a large brown arm and hand suddenly appeared, the hand being clapped heavily upon Mr. X's shoulder, whilst a gruff masculine voice asked him in loud tones, "Are you really satisfied?"

I have witnessed some strange happenings in connection with my investigation of occult matters, but to my dying day I shall never forget the look of blank astonishment on Mr. X's face at that moment.

Quickly recovering himself, however, he at once examined the Sensitive—a little woman, far below the average height, having small hands and feet, as we could all see quite clearly—and declared that every seal and every knot was unbroken, and just as he had left them not sixty seconds before.

Amongst other entities who materialized that evening was a young girl of about eighteen years of age, who stated that when she left her earth-body she had been a dancer at a café in Algiers.

She came from the spot where the Sensitive was seated, laughing heartily, stating that the hand and arm belonged to an old English sailor, whom she spoke of as "the Captain." She said, further, that he had been standing with her watching the tying-up process from their sphere, and laughing at Mr. X's vain attempt to prevent the production of the phenomena. The Captain had very much wished to materialize fully, so as to surprise Mr. X. as he stepped back from the Sensitive; but finding that he could only get sufficient "power" to produce a hand and arm, he was in a bad temper. And this was evidently the case, for during the ten minutes that the girl remained talking to us we could now and then hear the gruff voice of the Captain rolling out language which can only be described as "forcible and free."

The experiment lasted for nearly an hour, and at its conclusion Mr. X. examined the Sensitive, and once again reported that every seal and knot were just as he had left them at the commencement of the experiment.

EXPERIMENT No. 4

Place—my house in London. Sensitive D, male, aged about 34.

On numerous occasions this Sensitive has been seen by all present, in gaslight shaded by red paper, seated on his chair in a state of deep trance, and was heard to be breathing heavily, whilst two materialized entities stood beside him; or with one beside him, and the other standing five to eight feet away from him and close to the Sitters.

Again, two female entities were seen simultaneously when this (male) Sensitive was experimenting with us, one of them inside the half-circle formed by the sixteen Sitters, and talking to them in a low sweet voice, at a distance of about eight feet from the Sensitive; whilst the other female entity passed through or over the Sitters, and walking about the room outside the half-circle formed by the Sitters, came up behind two of them, and not only spoke audibly to them, but also held a short conversation with the entity inside the ring, both speaking almost instantaneously.

EXPERIMENT No. 5

Place—my house in London. Sensitive D, male, aged about 34.

One of the two female entities referred to in Experiment No. 4, a tall and particularly graceful woman, apparently about twenty-five years of age, was walking amongst the Sitters, talking to them, and showing them her beautifully modeled hands, the fingers being unusually long and tapering.

Stopping in front of one of the male Sitters (Mr. D.), whose thoughts at that moment she must have clearly read, she asked him to lend her his gold signet-ring. He admitted afterwards, that in spite of all that he saw for himself that night, he still half believed that the male Sensitive had escaped from his chair, and was masquerading cleverly as the female entity.

With considerable difficulty Mr. D. took the ring off his little finger, and she then held up both her hands, and in the presence of the fifteen other Sitters, she dropped his ring quite easily over, not only each of her eight fingers, but over both thumbs as well. He then put the ring into his waistcoat pocket, and at the conclusion of the experiment, we stood round him whilst he tested the ring on the hands of the Sensitive, and he was altogether unable to pass it over the second joint of any of his fingers on either hand, and could not get it on to his thumbs at all.

EXPERIMENT No. 6

Place—the Psychological Society, London. Sensitive C, male, aged about 50.

This Sensitive is the one to whom I referred on page 27, the man who would not sit apart from the circle formed by the Sitters, but insisted on sitting amongst them, two of them holding his hands firmly with their own during the whole time that we were experimenting with him. He did not pass into a state of trance, but was perfectly normal during the experiment, and when a materialized form appeared he would speak to the entity inhabiting the form as it moved about the room, and the entity would reply in a clear voice, which was distinctly audible, not only to the fourteen or sixteen Sitters in the room, but to two observers who were stationed outside the door of the room, whose notes, made at the time, proved conclusively that we were none of us hallucinated during the experiment.

On the occasion to which I now refer, the organist was absent owing to illness, so the harmonium was closed, and a circle bf Sitters was formed at a distance of twenty feet away from the instrument; and there the Sensitive sat, firmly held by the two officials in charge of him for that night—the president and vice-president of the society.

In about ten minutes a tall and slim man appeared in our midst, who after passing mysteriously either through or over the circle formed by the Sitters, walked slowly to the harmonium, raised the cover, and pushed it back. He then seated himself on the music-stool, and drawing out some of the stops, played half a dozen perfectly harmonious chords upon the instrument, using both hands, and apparently working the pedals with both feet.

The music was distinctly heard, not only by the fourteen Sitters present in the room, but also by the two observers stationed outside the room; the Sensitive being held securely during the whole time that the experiment lasted, at a distance of nearly twenty feet away from the entity seated upon the music-stool.

Half an hour later, one of the entities suggested that a little music would help to make the conditions better. So I left my seat, went to the harmonium and was in the act of playing a voluntary, when the Sensitive, nearly twenty feet away, said, "Look behind you, please." I turned my head, and there almost touching me, stood the same tall and slender figure of a man; and gazing closely into his face, I at once perceived that his features were of a distinctly different type to those of the Sensitive, whilst his height exceeded that of the Sensitive by nearly three inches. He said, "We thank you, friend, for your kind help: the vibrations given off by this instrument are of very great assistance to us during these delicate experiments."

EXPERIMENT No. 7

Place—Whitehall, London. S. W. Sensitive D, male, aged about 34.

Two young men, to whom I shall refer as Mr. T. and Mr. W., who had often experimented with this Sensitive at my house in London, asked him if he would attend at their "office" one evening to see if any results could be obtained there; and he at once accepted their offer, and they were good enough to invite me to join their party of friends.

Today those two young men are holding high positions in the State, but they had never allowed the fact to leak out that they were in any way connected with the Government or its Services, and from their reference to the "office" we all assumed that they were engaged in business in London.

They asked me to bring the Sensitive to an address which they gave me, and on driving to this address with him, I saw that it was a narrow street leading out of that busy thoroughfare, Whitehall (London); and on stopping the cab, I was greatly surprised to find that we were drawn up at (apparently) the side entrance to a very large building, the front of which evidently faced Whitehall.

Before I had time to say a word to the Sensitive, or to draw his attention to what I had seen of the building, Mr. T. and Mr. W.

hurried down the steps leading to it and ushered us into a splendid entrance-hall, up a palatial staircase, and into a very large and lofty room, beautifully decorated and furnished in sumptuous style with massive writing-desks, large chairs and settees upholstered in scarlet leather, whilst on the floor was a carpet into which our boots sank luxuriously. Two ladies were waiting for us near the handsomely carved fireplace, and we were then informed that no other persons had been invited: so closing and locking the doors, we took our seats round the Sensitive in one corner of the palatial room and awaited results.

Now, in this instance again, little or no special preparation had been made for the experiment, and, in spite of the splendor of the place and its contents, I told them that I doubted if we should get anything whatever in the way of results under such adverse conditions.

The Sensitive quickly passed into a state of trance, and, in less than fifteen minutes of our taking our seats, the figure of a tall and elderly man appeared, who stooped slightly as he walked. He moved towards Mr. T. and Mr. W., who recognized him instantly; the ladies too both recognized him; but as no name was mentioned by them, I concluded that the entity was probably a relative or personal friend of theirs.

After standing before them for nearly two minutes, he suddenly turned and walked up to within eighteen inches of the spot where I was seated. I knew him at a glance, and said, "Why, it is Lord ___ whom I so often saw in 1881." He at once bowed his head and smiled at me in quite a friendly way, but although his lips moved distinctly, I did not hear what he said.

Mr. T. was the first to speak aloud. He said, "This is more than wonderful. The place in which we are sitting is the __ __(London), and this is Lord __'s own room. We decided to sit here as a test, without telling you or the Sensitive the place we had selected, in order that we might see whether it was possible for Lord __ to return to the room which he so dearly loved, the one in which so many of his greatest diplomatic triumphs were carried to a successful issue." They then told me for the first time that they were both in the Service.

Two or three other entities appeared; and a small wild animal from India, to which I shall refer shortly, also materialized, in spite of my imploring the entities not to let him do so, or at least to keep him in check in such a palatial apartment. But this the entities declared themselves incapable of doing and the little animal scampered into the room, climbed on to the gorgeous writing-desk nearest to us, and rushed across it, scattering official papers, pens, and pencils in wild confusion.

How we all escaped the headsman's block on Tower Hill, or imprisonment for life, for our escapade in a Government building, and in one of the most sacred rooms in that building, remains an unsolved mystery to me to this day!

EXPERIMENT No. 8

Place—Wilton Crescent, London, S. W. Sensitive D, male, aged about 34.

Whilst this (male) Sensitive was seated in a corner of the room, and wedged in there tightly by the ring of Sitters grouped round him—Sitter No.1 being not more than three feet from him—

a female entity appeared, who at once walked out amongst the Sitters and stood talking to them for more than five minutes. When at a distance of about eight feet from the Sensitive, one of the legs of the wooden chair on which he was seated suddenly gave way, and he fell forward into my arms, as I happened to be the Sitter No. 1 and nearest to him. He was in deep trance, breathing heavily and groaning slightly.

Contrary to our expectations, the entity was not nearly so startled as were the Sitters, her first thought being for him. She stood perfectly still at the spot where she had been at the moment of the accident, and directly we had propped up the chair temporarily, and had placed the unconscious Sensitive upon the seat once more, she walked slowly towards him and then de-materialized, as she often used to do, passing to all appearances through the floor.

This was always an interesting portion of the experiment to watch. The feet and ankles would first disappear; then slowly the legs, up to the hips, would sink downwards; next the body up to the neck; followed—after a few words of farewell—by the face, the top of the head remaining for about thirty seconds on the surface of the floor, the dazzling white of the drapery, in which the head had been draped during the appearance of the entity in our midst, showing plainly above the dark-colored carpet. The dematerialization lasted for about a minute and a quarter from first to last, and was clearly visible, by artificial light, to all present on every occasion.

EXPERIMENT No. 9

Place—Eaton Square, London, S. W. Sensitive D, male, aged about 34.

Materializations of both beasts and birds sometimes appeared during our experiments with this Sensitive, the largest and most startling being that of a seal, which appeared on one occasion when Field-Marshal Lord Wolseley was present.

The first time that this occurred was in a private house in Eaton Square, which the Sensitive had never entered before, the owner of the house being a complete stranger to him at the time.

During the experimental meeting we suddenly heard a remarkable voice calling out some absurd remarks in loud tones, finishing off with a shrill whistle. "Why, that must be our old parrot," said the lady of the house. "He lived in this room for many years, and would constantly repeat those very words." This was at once confirmed by her daughter, and also by the lady's governess, who were present as Sitters.

As this was the first occasion on which I had ever even heard of such a thing as the materialization of a beast or bird, I was completely nonplussed for the moment, I confess; but one of the entities explained the matter to us, and after that evening we occasionally witnessed materializations of some of the badly-named "lower orders" of creation.

Both scientific and lay critics, who up to this stage of our investigation had merely termed us hallucinated cranks (just as they had termed Sir William Crookes), now stated boldly that we were either descendants of Ananias and Sapphira or else as mad as March hares. But the results of the next experiment which I will record disposed of these criticisms finally, for I was able to prove the truth of my assertions by ocular demonstration to many of our would-be critics.

A small wild animal from India—the at one time pet of a lady present on the occasion to which I shall now refer, an animal which had been "dead" for three years or more, and had never been seen or heard of by the Sensitive, and was known to only one other Sitter—suddenly ran out from the spot where the Sensitive was sitting, breathing heavily and in a state of deep trance, the little creature uttering exactly the same cry which it had always used as a sign of pleasure during its earth-life. The entities told us not to be alarmed at its appearance, as it would take on its old conditions, and would be quite harmless.

It had shown itself altogether on about ten different occasions, staying in the room for not more than two minutes at a time, and then disappearing just as suddenly as it had arrived upon the scene. But on this occasion, the lady who had owned it during its life called it to her by its pet name, and it then proceeded to climb slowly up on to her lap.

Resting there quietly for about half a minute, it then attempted to return, but in doing so caught one of its legs in the lace with which the lady's skirt was covered. It struggled violently, and at last got itself free, but not until it had torn the lace for nearly three inches, as was afterwards discovered. At the conclusion of the experiment, a medical man (Dr A. C.) who was present asked everyone to remain in their seats whilst he made a careful inspection of the torn lace. He reported that there were five green-colored hairs hanging in the torn lace, which had evidently become detached from the little animal's leg during its struggles. The lady at once identified the color and the texture of the hairs, and this was confirmed by the other Sitter—himself a naturalist—who had frequently seen and handled the animal during its earth-life.

The five hairs were carefully collected, placed in tissue paper, and then shut up in a light-tight and damp-proof box. They were shown to several scientific and other investigators in London; but after a few days they commenced to dwindle in size, and finally disappeared entirely, owing, we assume, to the action of the actinic rays given off by the daylight and the gaslight when they were being inspected by inquirers.

It was those five little green hairs which settled the sneers of our would-be critics finally.

Permission has been given occasionally by the entities to cut off with scissors a portion of the drapery so generally worn by them when making use of a materialized body; and if carefully preserved in a suitable box, it has been found possible to keep it for a short time, provided that the drapery was examined only in a non-actinic light. But in spite of the box being locked up in a safe, the material has always decreased in size, eventually disappearing entirely, and in consequence of this, I do not believe that it has ever been possible to make a scientific examination of it.

EXPERIMENT No. 10

Place—my house in London. Sensitive B, female, aged about 49.

The results of this experiment were, so far as I am personally concerned, the most wonderful, and at the same time the most convincing of all the tests which I have obtained.

Experimenting with a picked set of Sitters in my own room (with Sir William Crookes' Sensitive), the French dancing-girl was standing fully materialized from head to foot, barely six feet away from me, three or four feet away from the Sensitive, and directly opposite the gas-bracket; the flame being turned up to its full height, the light being only slightly shaded with a piece of yellow paper, in order that the direct rays from the gas might be somewhat softened before falling upon her, as otherwise her features would soon begin to melt and to run, exactly in the way that soft wax will melt in the presence of heat—an extremely painful and unpleasant sight to witness, as I know by experience.

She had been talking to us for five minutes, and showing us as usual her hands and arms, feet and legs, as she was evidently extremely proud of their beautiful modeling—when she turned to me and asked me to leave my seat and come and stand beside her. I did this, and she at once moved up quite close to me and rested her little head upon my right shoulder. I noticed that, although her features appeared to be smaller than those of a normal young woman of her age on earth, she was considerably taller than the Sensitive, then a rather short and stout woman of nearly fifty, and the mother of two grown-up daughters. Her complexion was beautifully fair, whilst that of the Sensitive was very dark, the hair in each case following the general coloring. Her ears were unpierced, while the Sensitive always wore earrings. These things satisfied me that the entity and the Sensitive were two absolutely separate beings. But not content with this, I, for the first and only time during the seven years which I devoted to this investigation, broke conditions: but the desire to settle the great problem once and for all so overmastered me that I very gently passed my right arm completely round the entity, and found that I was clasping the thin waist of a young girl, which felt both warm and firm to the touch through the white drapery with which it was covered; the measurement certainly not exceeding fifteen to sixteen inches, whereas the waist measurement of the Sensitive that night was twenty-four inches.

In this way, then, I received my final test, a test so absolutely convincing that I never asked for another one; and although I continued my investigations for several years longer, and with five other Sensitives, no entity ever gave me such a test as this, nor did I consider it necessary to ask them for another one.

But our red-letter evening was not yet over by any means, for instead of displaying anger at my breaking conditions so deliberately, the entity merely smiled at the Sitters as I held her firmly in my grasp for half a minute or more, and did not attempt to take her head from my shoulder until I had released her from my grasp. I then apologized to her for what I had done, and thanking her for giving me so wonderful a test, I returned to my seat.

She then invited a lady to take her stand beside her, singling out one who up to that moment had always candidly admitted that she regarded this special Sensitive as a fraud.

The lady left her seat, and stood close to the entity, who at once rested her head upon the lady's shoulder, permitting her to place her arm round the girl's waist; and a very charming picture they made, the lady being dressed in a modern evening costume, the girlish form of the entity being clad in flowing robes of dazzling whiteness. They stood like this for nearly a minute, when we heard the entity ask the lady to turn her head round, and to look at the spot where the Sensitive was sitting in deep trance, only about four feet away.

She did this, and stated that she could see the Sensitive distinctly, her head drooping upon her chest, her arms and hands hanging loosely at her sides, and her body clothed in black velvet; for she always insisted on wearing not only a black dress during our experiments with her, but black underclothing throughout, even giving to us her pocket-handkerchief just before she passed into trance, so that no one could ever accuse her of masquerading as a materialized entity clad in white robes.

Sir William Crookes carried out a series of experiments with this Sensitive, Florrie Cook, before her marriage to Mr. Corner, and she lived in the house of Sir William and Lady Crookes, in London, for some years, I believe.

Needless to say, the experiments which he conducted were always carried out under the very strictest test conditions which a man of such world-wide renown as a scientist could devise; and it was owing to the splendid training which she obtained under Sir William Crookes that she was able to produce, during my experiments with her, long after her marriage, such wonderful materializations in strong light, and after submitting willingly to a searching examination of her clothes and body by a qualified medical man. Instead of shrinking from tests, she was always glad to think that we were endeavoring to obtain them through her; and when we had succeeded, no one was more thoroughly gratified to hear of our good fortune than Mrs. Corner herself. All honor to her memory.

During Sir William Crookes' experiments with her, an entity, calling herself "Katie," permitted him not only to cut off portions of the white drapery in which she always appeared, and a long lock of hair from her head, but permitted him to hold her in his arms and to make a scientific examination of her materialized body.

He writes in the public press: "Having seen so much of Katie lately when she has been illuminated by the electric light, I am able to add to the points of difference between her and the Sensitive which I mentioned in a former article. I have the most absolute certainty that the Sensitive and Katie are two separate individuals so far as their bodies are concerned. Katie's neck was bare last night, the skin was perfectly smooth both to touch and sight, whilst on the Sensitive's neck is a large blister, which under similar circumstances is distinctly visible and rough to the touch. Katie's complexion is very fair, while that of the Sensitive is very dark. Last night, with bare feet and not 'tip-toeing,' Katie was four and a half inches taller than the Sensitive. The Sensitive's hair is so dark a brown as almost to appear black. A lock of Katie's hair, which is now before me, and which she allowed me to cut from her luxurious tresses, having first traced it up to the scalp and satisfied myself that it actually grew there, is a rich golden auburn."

In another published report he states that he timed Katie's pulse on one occasion. It beat steadily at seventy-five, whilst on timing the Sensitive's pulse he found that it was going at its usual rate of ninety. He applied his ear to Katie's chest and could hear a heart beating steadily inside, and pulsating even more steadily than the Sensitive's heart. Katie's lungs too he tested, and found them to be sounder than those of the Sensitive, who at that time was under medical treatment for a severe cough.

Katie, on one occasion, walked about the room fully materialized for nearly two hours, conversing familiarly with the Sitters present. Asking him to come to her, she took Sir William

Crookes' arm, and walked about the room with him arm in arm, the impression conveyed to his mind being that he was escorting a living woman instead of an entity from another sphere, so perfect was the materialization.

He states that on the occasion on which the greatest test of all was given to him, Katie asked him to leave the other Sitters and to come with her to the spot where the Sensitive was lying in a state of deep trance. He found her crouching on the floor dressed in black velvet, as she had been when the experiment commenced, and to all appearance perfectly senseless. He looked round, and saw Katie standing close to the Sensitive: she was robed, as always, in flowing white drapery. He then took hold of the Sensitive's hands, and kneeling down, carefully examined Katie so as to satisfy himself that it was actually her, and was not a phantasm or an hallucination. Katie did not speak during the examination, but only moved her head and smiled.

Three separate times did he carefully and critically examine the Sensitive crouching on the floor before him, to make certain that the hand which he held in his was that of a living woman; and three separate times did he examine Katie, "with steadfast scrutiny," as he so well says, until he had no doubt whatever as to her objective reality: the reality of her presence beside him.

At last the Sensitive moved slightly, and Katie instantly motioned him to go away. He moved a short distance from the Sensitive, and then ceased to see Katie, but he did not leave the spot until the Sensitive woke up.

Thus we see that Sir William Crookes handled both the entity and the Sensitive simultaneously, three separate times.

So careful was he as to little details that he actually arranged for a friend who could write shorthand to be close to him during this test, in order that he might take down word for word everything that he reported at the moment during the test.

He not only photographed Katie and the Sensitive together, but after asking permission, he clasped the materialized entity in his arms and found, as I did, that he was holding as solid a being as the Sensitive herself.

As President of the British Association he boldly declared before all the world that, after more than a quarter of a century, there was no statement which he had made upon this subject that he wished to retract or to alter in the light of later experience. As President of the Royal Society he stands today as one of the great leaders of the world of science, and this in spite of the persecution that he endured for years, on account of his candid declaration of the proved existence of these entities in materialized bodies, at the hands of men of whom it has been well said they were not worthy to untie his shoe-laces. The high position to which he has attained is a sufficient guarantee of his clearness and accuracy as an observer, his wide experience as a scientific investigator, the soundness of his judgment, and above all, the probity of his character, which in a matter of this kind is of the very first importance.

* * * * *

In the face of solid facts, such as I have recorded here, is it any wonder that I and those who assisted me in my investigations, supported as we are by the evidence of Sir William Crookes, Professor Alfred Russel Wallace, and other master scientists, should declare positively that we have both seen and handled entities from another sphere, who have taken upon themselves materialized bodies temporarily: seeing with their eyes: hearing with their ears: speaking and singing with their lips, just as you or I, or any other normal human being, can do?

It would be rank cowardice on my part were I to keep silence any longer as to the results which I obtained during the seven years which I devoted to a critical investigation of this, the most wonderful of all the phenomena offered for our investigation by these entities from another sphere, and I intend to keep silence no longer, come what may. I am fully aware of the consequences of making statements such as those recorded here, for scientific and lay critics alike poured whole volumes of abuse upon Sir William Crookes' head for daring to make public the results of his experiments in materializations; and I have not the slightest doubt but that the same narrow-minded, pettifogging, carping spirit will be found amongst those today who cannot believe the facts which I have related here: facts which are proven up to the hilt: facts which no amount of argument, no amount of quibbling or distortion can ever move a single hair's-breadth.

For scientists to scoff at the idea of entities from another sphere taking on temporary bodies, and working under certain clearly defined conditions, is merely to display childish and willful ignorance: and until they take the trouble to investigate these matters for themselves, and to listen to what the entities have to tell us concerning their life in the spheres in which they dwell, they are not entitled to pronounce an off-hand judgment, still less an injurious judgment, on the labors of those who, perhaps with fewer qualifications, but certainly with an equal desire of getting at the truth, have cheerfully undertaken the cost and the labor of the investigation, which they themselves have willfully neglected.

* * * * *

HYPNOTISM

The suggestion has frequently been made in the Press and elsewhere, that we were all hypnotized during our experiments. The reply to this suggestion is, that collective hypnotism is proved conclusively to be impossible. By incessant practice on the same individuals only, I find that I can obtain control over (say) three to five out of twelve really good subjects. In our case, however, the sixteen sitters were changed at practically every experiment, so that it would have been impossible to have induced the hypnotic condition in more than one or two simultaneously.

Hypnotism in any shape or form should be strictly forbidden in connection with such delicate experiments as those under consideration; and to deliberately place a Sensitive under hypnotic influence at the commencement of an experimental meeting, instead of permitting him to pass voluntarily into genuine trance, is simply courting disaster so far as results are concerned. This has been proved conclusively in France and Germany recently, where on passing a Sensitive for materializations into the hypnotic sleep, the forms issuing from the Sensitive in many instances so strongly resembled illustrations in current numbers of local newspapers— which had been seen by the operator or some of the experimenters (or both), and had deeply impressed themselves upon the brains (and minds) of those present—that whilst more advanced investigators at once discern the cause of the trouble, the vast majority, in a state of utter bewilderment through their inexperience, put the results down to fraud on the part of the entirely innocent Sensitive.

CHAPTER 4
QUESTIONS ANSWERED BY VARIOUS ENTITIES

SPHERES

Q. We often hear you use the word "Spheres." Can you give us any information concerning them: their number, for instance, where they are situated, and if you can pass from one to the other at will?

A. Their exact number I cannot tell you, but I will endeavor to answer the other portions of your question to the best of my ability. We find it extremely difficult to explain matters of this kind to you, on account of the limitations of your languages on earth; and are therefore forced to use terms and illustrations which will make our explanation simple, although perhaps not giving to you quite so full or so accurate a description as we should wish.

Now, to deal with your question. It is sufficient for you as mortals to know of "the seven spheres of active life" which succeed your earth-life.

The earth as you now know is round and you can therefore picture to yourselves these seven spheres as grouped round it in ever-widening circles. Do not smile at my reminding you that your earth is round, for you cannot have forgotten that in consequence of the absurd teaching in your sacred writings every Christian and Jew, including all the men of science, until about five hundred years ago, was firmly convinced that the earth was flat, and all who taught that it was round were punished with "death."

The sphere or plane of dynamic energy nearest to earth, you can call the first sphere, and this is the one to which the majority of mortals are attracted when they pass out of their earth-bodies, and commence their life of progress—or the reverse—in "the spheres of active life."

But those amongst you who have forever cast off the shackles of all the false creeds and dogmas of earth; you who are making good progress along the free and open road of spiritual knowledge—"the enlightened ones," as we call you—should make it your endeavor to so live your lives here and now, that when you leave your earth-body for the last time you should at once pass through this First Sphere without pause; should open your eyes in the Second Sphere, having left all undesirable earth-conditions behind you forever as you passed from earth. Let this, then, be your aim during the few years of life on this planet which still remain to you.

There is with us a fixed and immutable law that we may all pass downwards, as you would say, to the sphere or spheres below the one in which we are living, and when we choose to do so, just as I have done tonight in coming to meet you here; but none can pass upwards, as you would say, to the sphere or spheres above them, until the appointed hour has arrived for each entity to do so.

We often hear you quote the words of your poet, "there is no death." That is perfectly true so far as regards the views you hold concerning the change which takes place at the end of your earth-life, and which you term "death"—a change, by the way, which is identical with the one which occurs at the commencement of your earth-life, and which you term "birth."

But, although there is no "death" in the sense in which you employ that word, either in your sphere or in ours, something analogous to it occurs with each of us in our sphere when the appointed hour for our transition to a higher one arrives; for on opening our eyes, after passing through this change, we find ourselves in a far grander sphere than the one which we have left, no matter how beautiful, how perfect, that sphere may have appeared to us to be.

And this will continue, we understand, throughout the ages; each entity progressing in its sphere until the period of training in that sphere is completed, when it at once passes to the next sphere above them: progressing ever upwards. We can always return to the spheres below us, as I have already said, but we can never pass to a sphere above us until our appointed hour arrives.

You will find this well described in the book, Through the Mists, which one of us gave to you people of earth through the brain and hand of Robert James Lees.

SPIRITUALISATION OF MATTER

Q. Can you explain to us how the materialized bodies which are used during our experiments are formed?

A. The elements which go to make up the human, animal, and floral envelopes or bodies for the life-spirit contained in each of them are held in solution in the atmosphere, and can—through a knowledge of the laws governing it—be used to construct instantaneously any of the multitudinous forms that exist in nature; and it would be as easy for us to produce a materialization of an elephant in your midst, as a human being, provided that the conditions were favorable.

It was the knowledge of these laws which made many so-called "miracles" possible in the past—such as those recorded in your sacred writings (Bible)—and make many so-called "miracles" possible today.

This knowledge is possessed by those in our sphere who are adopts in chemistry, and who act as leaders during all experiments for the spiritualization of matter—not, as you term it, the materialization of Spirits, for it is far other than this.

The Sensitive is but another source from whom the elements for the materialized bodies can be drawn, for the atmosphere is not always chemically favorable.

At times, owing to unsuitable conditions, it is absolutely impossible to get together, even from both these sources—the atmosphere and the Sensitive—sufficient material with which to build up a body; and then, if forms still appear in your midst, the manifestation ceases to be a materialization and becomes a transfiguration. By this we mean that the Sensitive is transfigured, as a sculptor might modify an old statue with his chisel instead of forming a new figure from fresh materials. In transfigurations the face of the Sensitive is completely changed by the controlling entity, so as to represent his (the entity's) face temporarily. The unconscious Sensitive is then brought from his chair and walks amongst the Sitters, stopping before each of them, and showing his altered, transfigured features to them, as you know, by means of large pieces of cardboard, termed "the slates," which have previously been coated with luminous paint, as transfigurations when substituted for materializations usually occur in perfect darkness only.

In transfigurations then the Sensitive's face, changed in form and feature as if it had been melted and run into a new mold, is used to personate something quite as honest as the materialization for which it is so often mistaken; and all who attend your experimental meetings should be fully instructed beforehand as to the difference between these phenomena, and why it is that the leaders of the experiments in our sphere are sometimes compelled to produce transfigurations instead of the materializations which you expect to see.

Spiritualization of matter is governed by certain natural laws, and, like all such laws, they are immutable, i.e. absolutely unchangeable. The work of the true investigator should be to discover the operation of these laws, and to regulate his investigations accordingly.

When you speak of anything whatever as a "miracle," you imply that you actually know all natural laws; and when something occurs which you cannot by any possibility explain, instead of endeavoring to discover under what—to you—new natural law the apparently impossible has become possible, you foolishly say, "This is something quite beyond all natural laws, and is therefore a 'miracle'."

SPIRIT, SOUL, AND BODY

Q. (By G. B.) In the fifteenth chapter of the first letter to the Corinthians in the Christian Bible, we read of "a spiritual body". Can you explain this to us?

A. "Man—Woman—know Thyself." Man IS a spirit now and throughout the ages: and HAS a soul (or Spiritual-body) now and for a portion of his life beyond the grave: and HAS a material, physical, or earth-body during his life on earth, which he leaves behind him there forever, at the change which you term "death."

In the letter to which you refer, the writer is dealing with this, the greatest of all the trinities in your sphere, Psyche, pneuma, soma (Spirit, soul, and body), "the three in one" which form Life in the earth-sphere: for, wherever there is life, there also is Spirit: where there is Spirit, there also is soul (or spiritual-body) so long as the earth-life lasts, and for a certain period in the spheres as well: where there is Spirit on the earth-sphere there also is a material body, which is left behind forever at the "death" of that body.

You will remember that in the thirty-fifth verse in that chapter the writer refers to the question so often asked, "How are the dead raised up, and with what body do they come?"

He replies, "Thou foolish one, the seed which thou sowest (in the ground) is not quickened (endued with life) except it (first) die: and that which thou sowest, thou sowest not that body that shall be, but bare grain—it may happen to be wheat or some other grain: but God giveth it a body as it hath pleased Him, and to every seed his own body."

The insignificant looking grain of wheat is put into the ground, leaves its body there forever, but the Spirit, the Life, contained within that little seed, rises from the ground a tall and graceful stalk, bearing well-filled ears of corn.

"So also," he continues, "is the resurrection of the dead." The earth or natural-body is sown in corruption: the spiritual-body (soul) is raised in incorruption. The natural-body is sown in dishonor: the spiritual-body (soul) is raised in glory. The natural-body is sown in weakness: the spiritual-body (soul) is raised in power. Mark this carefully: "It is sown a natural-body; it is raised a spiritual-body. There IS a natural-body, and there IS a spiritual-body."

And yet, in the face of such teaching as this, Christianity dares to proclaim the resurrection of the earth or physical body!

By another entity. You and we are now and always immortal Spirits, and you are visiting the earth, as a part of your spiritual evolution, for a period of training and discipline, and you are Spirits clothed, during this period, with an earth or physical-body and a spiritual-body (soul), and each one of you is therefore a complete "trinity in unity," as has been said, in him or herself, formed as you are at this moment of Spirit, spiritual-body, and earth or physical-body.

And, just as at the change which you term "birth," at the commencement of your earth-life, the Spirit became clothed upon with its spiritual-body and developed its earth-body—so, at the change which you term "death," at the termination of your earth-life, the Spirit, still clad in its spiritual-body, will pass out of your earth-body, which it then leaves for ever; and passing upwards during the ages from one sphere to another, it will gradually part with more and more of its spiritual-body at each step upwards, until at length, and as pure Spirit only, it will return to God, who IS Spirit.

In proportion as the Spirit progresses in the spheres, the essence of its spiritual-body, which consists of the finer nervous fluids, becomes more and more etherealized; whence it follows that the influence of matter diminishes in exact proportion to the advancement of the Spirit, i.e., the spiritual-body becomes less and less gross, and consequently more and more spiritual, as the Spirit within it progresses.

By another entity. The real YOU, altogether invisible to normal human sight, rests at this moment within two separate and quite distinct envelopes or bodies: the one visible to normal sight, the material or earth-body, controlled by its brain; the other invisible to normal sight, although plainly visible to clairvoyant sight', the spiritual body, controlled by its spiritual replica of the brain, the mind.

As was well said in one of your psychic journals recently—although I shall venture to make a few slight additions—" The spiritual-body consists of finer ether, and has a mind (consciousness), as distinct a thing from the brain as this spiritual-body is from the earth-body, but they are inhabitants of another sphere. And you can slip this finer body, with its mind, out of your physical body; and after death it is just the same in appearance as during life.

"This spiritual-body started its career at the moment you started being made by your microscopic father (spermatozoon) and mother (ovum). It is their offspring, as essentially as you are. It did not exist before you: it has no chance to be self-existent or immortal, like your Spirit. It had a natural beginning, as you had, and therefore from a normal point of view must have an end (and eventually does), but its dissolution does not occur at the time of the death of your earth-body, for it survives this," and gradually becomes less and less as you, as Spirit, progress upwards through the spheres.

Many mortals seem to think that at birth you came to earth straight from your Deity—or, as you Christians say, from "heaven" to earth—and that at death you will return straight to your Deity—or, as you Christians say, to "heaven" or "hell," according to the lives you have lived whilst on earth.

Now "heaven" and "hell," I would remind you, are not places above, below, or around you; but are states or conditions in your earth-life, and also in your life and ours in the spheres; and you and we make our own "heaven" or our own "hell," according to the lives you and we lead in our respective spheres.

You will find that the human Spirit, far from coming straight to earth from "heaven," has lived on many planets or worlds before it reached this one; just as it will live in many spheres after its period of training on earth is ended.

Myriads of worlds swarm in space, and in a certain number of these worlds each Spirit in rudimental conditions performs a portion of its pilgrimage ere it reaches this little planet called "earth"; and it is the function of this world to confer upon the Spirit the consciousness of itself, and knowledge of good and evil. Only whilst on earth is the Spirit man or woman; prior to this, in every other stage of its vast journey, it has been but an embryonic being, a fleeting temporary form of matter, gaining here a little and there a little; a creature in which is a portion of the high imprisoned Spirit-seed which shines forth in a rudimental shape with rudimental functions, as a butterfly springing up from the chrysalis; ever going onward into new life, new death, living and dying, stretching and reaching upward, striving onward along the pathways of life in the planets.

At last comes the day when it awakens to find itself a thing encased in a material body for the first time, to find itself a creature of flesh and blood for a short period termed "the earth-life"—a man or a woman.

After this birth of the Spirit—(encased in its soul or spiritual-body)—in a material or earth- body, it acquires the knowledge of its own individuality, its passions, its loves, and a knowledge of good and evil: it gains self-consciousness, and in doing these things, is closing forever its career of material pilgrimage and transformation.

With the death of the earth-body, the Spirit (still clad in its spiritual-body) at once gravitates to a fresh series of pilgrimages and existences in our spheres, the realms of Spirit: and here begin the further purification and growth of the Spirit, now filled—by its experience gained during the earth-life—with either the sublime attributes of Love and Wisdom gained by self-knowledge, or with the lower attributes of the animal by which it permitted itself to be conquered or overcome during its earth-life. Hence the vital importance of the warning which we so often give to you men and women of earth to loosen the ties, especially the animal ties, which would tend to hold you to earth after you have passed out of your physical bodies for the last time.

Q. (By another Sitter, A. D.) You say, "When you leave your earth-body for the last time." Do we then, ever leave our bodies during our lives on earth?

A. (By a medical entity.) Yes, constantly; for practically every night of your life, you, the real you (the Spirit A. D.), and all normal men and women, pass a portion of each night just outside your earth-bodies after you (the Spirit A. D.) have had sufficient rest; say, from about two and a half to three and a half hours, according to the amount of work, and the kind of work, mental or physical, which the earth-body and its brain has performed during the day. For this reason a human being of any age should never be awakened suddenly from their sleep, for the shock to both spirit and body is a very severe one indeed; the most dangerous hours, in my opinion, being those from midnight to about four o'clock in the morning.

"The enlightened ones" amongst you, those who have made real progress in spiritual matters, are often able to remember what they have both seen and heard whilst as Spirits, and fully conscious themselves, they stood beside their unconscious earth-bodies lying on the bed before them, wrapped in healthy slumber. There is little or no fear of persons like these coming to any harm, such as being murdered or burnt to death during their sleep, for the spirit standing outside their body acts as a sentry; and passing gently but swiftly back into the body at the first sign of danger, rouses it from its state of insensibility into one of immediate action.

On the other hand, the men and women who fill their bodies with indigestible food, or saturate themselves with alcohol just before retiring to their beds, make it almost impossible for the Spirit to detach itself from their body during the heavy stupor which, in their case, takes the place of natural sleep; and these are the persons who are injured or killed during the night, for the simple reason that the poor crushed Spirit within their gorged bodies has been rendered useless as a sentry to guard them during their slumbers.

It seems to me that most of you men and women of the white races on earth spend your time, instead of trying to develop your spiritual nature—your real mission whilst on earth—in trying to dig your graves with your teeth; for diet plays a far more important part in your earth-life than you have any idea of at present.

It is truly marvelous to those of us in the spheres who are interested in what you term scientific subjects, how ignorant you men and women are concerning your bodies. "Man—Woman—know THYSELF" is a saying which all should take seriously to heart.

In a few moments now I shall return to my own sphere, and were I then to meet a scientist who knew nothing concerning the people of earth, and to tell him that I had just left men and women who deemed themselves well educated, and yet had little or no knowledge of the organs contained within their bodies, such as the spleen, for instance, he would stare at me in blank amazement; and were I to tell him further that the surgeons and physicians of earth had little or no knowledge concerning such vitally important organs as the solar plexus and the pineal gland—the difference between brain and mind—absolutely nothing whatever concerning human polarity; and were firmly convinced that all normal persons breathed through both nostrils simultaneously—he would regard the condition of such scientists as one bordering on lunacy.

Q. (By Dr A. C.) I admit that we know but little concerning the solar plexus and the pineal gland, and nothing whatever about human polarity; whilst your suggestion as to normal human breathing is an entirely new one to me. Can you throw any light upon these matters?

A. Your polarity changes each two hours (or thereabouts) from positive to negative or vice versa, and your breathing changes with it. From the moment of "birth" to the moment of "death" every normal human being breathes through only one nostril at a time, and that for a period of two hours (or thereabouts), when the breathing changes over to the other nostril for a period of two hours (or thereabouts), the only time that it passes through both nostrils simultaneously being the moment when the polarity and the breathing are changing: the nostril through which a person is breathing at any given moment showing that it is the positive side of that person at the time. Try this little experiment for yourself, by breathing on to the hand, and try it again in two-hours time, and, provided that you have no obstruction in the nostrils, you will at once be compelled to admit the truth of what I have told you.

Although you do not realize the fact as yet, mighty waves of magnetism pass continuously between the north and south poles of your earth; and strong Astral currents run around your earth in the plane of the equator, the northern current running from east to west, the southern from west to east.

From these Astral currents others descend to either pole, which produces the polarity of the magnetic needle, as well as its dip.

If you are wise you will arrange your sleeping apartments so that when you lie in bed your body shall lie directly in the line of the mighty waves of magnetism always, i.e. of course, with your face and the foot of your bed to the north; or, if that is impossible, then to the south; but never to the east or west.

Watch the restlessness of your children at night, when you have deliberately placed their little bodies in direct opposition to these mighty waves of magnetism by trying to force them to sleep with their faces to the east or west. See how again and again during their sleep they will endeavor to turn their little bodies round—for the Spirit within each one of them fully realizes your folly—so that they may lie north and south, so as to face the waves of magnetism, instead of east and west, as you have placed them, and in direct opposition to those waves. Try the experiment in your hospitals, in your nursing homes, and in your sick rooms, and see what happy results will follow; for if, as we in our sphere know well, mortals in the enjoyment of full health are seriously affected by constantly sleeping in direct opposition to these mighty waves, think what the results must be upon children or invalids; and many instances of curvature of the spine in children may be traced to this cause, through your ignorance of these facts.

We often smile as we hear "the un-enlightened ones" amongst you saying, "Isn't it wonderful! I can nearly always wake up at any hour I wish if the matter is an important one, and if I set my mind on it beforehand: wake almost to the very minute. It seems quite a 'miracle' to me."

Instead of being a "miracle," however, it was merely the working of a natural law of which the speaker clearly had no knowledge. All that happened was that, before going to sleep, the physical "brain" impressed upon the spiritual "mind" of his or her Spirit the fact that it was important that they should wake up at a certain hour. When that hour arrived, the Spirit standing outside the body wrapped in healthy slumber became aware of the fact through its "mind," and gently passed back into the body. The "mind" at once acted upon the "brain," and the sleeper awoke, considerably surprised, and wondering as usual how such a "miracle" could have happened to them again; never dreaming that it was the result merely of a natural law, working quite normally. Once again I repeat, "Man—Woman—know THYSELF."

THE CHANGE TERMED "DEATH"

Q. Assuming that you entities have once had an earth existence, you must have "died," as we say. Can you tell us anything concerning your experiences in connection with this change?

A. As one who has passed through it, I could tell you much concerning that change, both as regards (1) the actual leaving the body, and then as regards (2) the state of the Spirit immediately after it has freed itself from the body. But I prefer to let a scientist on earth describe (1) a death-bed scene, as witnessed by him: the result of an investigation into the subject, which he carried out on strictly scientific lines at our suggestion; and I prefer to do this in the hope of inducing some of you "enlightened ones" to try the experiment for yourselves, as it will indeed prove to be a revelation to you. I will then add a few remarks of my own concerning (2) the state of the freed Spirit on its awakening in the new life in the spheres.

Now, if you have not developed your powers of clairvoyance, you must take steps to do this, or else must induce it by artificial means, as the scientists, whose report I shall now give to you, did so successfully. Begin to experiment also with a special photographic apparatus, and so obtain a witness whose testimony would prove invaluable in an investigation of this kind.

And what is it that you will see with your artificially induced clairvoyance? What is it that the specially prepared photographic lens should record? One of the two scientists shall tell you in his own words.

"Remembering your oft-repeated assertion that one could see the Spirit take flight at the moment of dissolution, I was not contented in my past blind ignorance, where I so often professed to know so much.

"The time finally arrived when I had proper conditions of light, etc., where a man of more than ordinary spirituality was being called over to the great majority. I watched the hours go by, till the moment came when he was about to cease breathing, and a sudden tremor passing through his body announced that his hour had come.

"Now is our time,' I whispered to the friend who was assisting me. We passed our heads under the black cloth—a thin violet column of vapor, gathered into a soft cloud, apparently formed over and about the body. Particle seemed to seek particle, as if by some molecular attraction, until the outline of an object was clearly distinguishable. As it grew stronger, it seemed the vapory form of a man, rapidly assuming a more perfect shape, now pure and colorless as the most perfect crystal, having changed from the violet tinge.

"There was at this moment an awful stillness. An indescribable feeling came over both of us: our hearts seemed to stand still. Words are perfectly inadequate to express or describe our feelings. We bent our eyes intently upon the glass, until particle after particle came into the shapely form of the man we had known so well. It lay floating about a foot above the body, apparently moored by a slender cord to the breast of the corpse. The face was the face of the man, but far more peaceful and beautiful in expression; the eyes were closed, and the new form apparently seemed asleep.

"Through some impulse, both my friend and myself wished, as it were simultaneously, that he might awake, when the cord that held the form to the body parted, a gentle tremor passed through the beautiful form, every limb of which was a perfect mold; a violet flame was radiating over the heart, a kind look on the gentle face. He had lived his life unselfishly, as we knew, and was an unexceptionable man when he was with us. As his beautiful inner life united with the outer one, the perfect mold became a perfect man.

"It then arose in a standing position, cast one sorrowful look at the earth-body that lay so still, extending a hand towards it as if toy, 'Farewell, thou narrow house! I need thee no more,' gathered its forces into a little sphere, and passed out into the sunlight of the everlasting morrow.

"We are assured and know that our friend lives—that he is immortal, a living presence forever, and we conclude our report of our discovery by saying that we are both changed men. To us this life and this world appear entirely different since our experience."

* * * * *

I sincerely trust that the results obtained by these two scientists on your earth-planet may be the means of inducing some of you to try the experiment for yourselves; and I am in hopes that, ere long now, photographs of the passing of the Spirit clad in its spiritual-body from the earth-body, at the change which you term "death," may become so common amongst you, that even the very poorest may in this way be able to obtain so convincing a proof of the fact that "death is but the gateway to eternal Life."

And now let me add a few words of my own on this interesting subject. I endorse what has been so well said by these two scientists, for observations made by us prove that the Spirit, encased in its spiritual-body, disengages itself but slowly from the earth-body; the final severance of the cord which holds them to that body not taking place until long after the person has been certified as "dead" by his medical attendant.

During the first few moments which follows complete severance of the two bodies, the Spirit of an "unenlightened one" does not as a rule clearly understand the situation. He does not believe himself to be "dead," for he feels himself to be thoroughly alive. He sees his body before him, knows that it is his, yet does not understand that he is separated from it finally; and according to the spiritual growth of the detached spirit, either this state of indecision, or else a state of numb unconsciousness continues so long as there remains the slightest connection between the now empty shell (the earth-body) and the Spirit clad in its spiritual-body.

At times, when there has been a violent and strong desire in the individual not to die, the Spirit clad in its spiritual-body returns and settles over and about the upper part of the corpse, after its burial; and there it will often remain for days, weeks, months, and even years, and until the earth-body has entirely returned to dust. This is the explanation of those apparitions termed "churchyard ghosts," so frequently to be seen in your burial-grounds: the body-bound Spirit, clad in its spiritual-body, being quite unable for various reasons to separate itself from its decaying earth-body. It was on this account that the ancient Greek and the other highly cultivated and progressed nations of the past esteemed it a privilege beyond all others to be cremated after "death"; and we endorse that reasonable desire on their part. We would urge upon you to burn all bodies, more especially those of murderers and suicides, and thus assist to release the body-bound Spirit from the anguish, nay more, the horror, of witnessing its earth-body slowly decaying in the grave.

This unquenched thirst for life in the earth-body is a great power amongst "the unenlightened ones" after their "death," and has a creative force so potent that it frequently draws the Spirit back into contact with its earth-life, when it should have passed on to loftier spheres. Strive therefore to increase your spiritual knowledge, and to test the beauties of the Spirit-world during your earth-life, so that when your time of passing comes, a creative force and power may receive you, which, drawing you away from your envelope or earth-body, may at once waft you onward, upward, to the spheres of progress.

Herein lies one of the greatest mistakes of modern times in connection with this subject of "death." When the hour has come to an individual, and the Spirit is about to depart from its earth-body, through blindness and cruel ignorance, relatives and friends gather round the bedside, and by their tears and prayers endeavor to call back the departing Spirit to earth, just when it is fluttering like a caged bird to obtain its freedom. By and through this ignorance of nature's law, the Spirit of many a loved one has been made to hover about his grave for months, awaiting release by the slow disintegration of the particles which formed his earth-body.

I repeat therefore :—at the moment of "death" do not by your tears and prayers try to induce the Spirit not to leave his earth-body, and thus cause him to become bound to earth: and, after "death", burn all bodies, and so assist the Spirit to obtain its freedom.

ANIMALS

Q. (By G. B.) As one result of my investigations of the phenomena which you entities offer to us for that purpose, I have gradually lost all belief in such terms as "miraculous", "supernatural," and words of that description but I confess that the appearance of beasts and birds during our experiments has come as a tremendous surprise to me. How is it that this is possible?

A. (By a scientific entity.) In the cases which have come under your observation it was partially owing to your deep interest in animal life of all kinds, as a naturalist; but even more on account of the great affection which the animals who appear in your midst still feel for their late owners on earth, who happened to be present at the same time that you also were experimenting with us. That was the happy combination which drew them towards you.

The parrot, for instance, was devoted to the mistress of the house in which we were conducting our experiments, and also to one of her daughters, both of them being present in the very room in which the parrot had spent so many years of its life—whilst you also were present: the happy combination.

The little wild animal from India was equally devoted to his late mistress, and appears to her constantly, as you know, but always only when you are present: once more the happy combination. Love with them, as with us, masters all difficulties.

But how they manage to obtain the material for their temporary bodies I do not understand; temporary bodies which are such accurate replicas of those which they occupied when on earth that even, as you saw, the very color and texture of the hair which covered the body of the little animal during its life on earth is reproduced exactly on its temporary body.

Q. (By G. B.) You say that when inhabiting these temporary bodies the animals are entirely beyond your control. How is this?

A. Their actions are altogether independent of us. Whilst we are busily engaged in conducting our experiments with human entities who wish to materialize in your midst, the animals get into the room in some way which we do not understand, and which we cannot prevent: obtain, from somewhere, sufficient matter with which to build up temporary bodies; coming just when they choose; roaming about the room just as they please; and disappearing just when it suits them, and not before; and we have no power to prevent this so long as the affection existing between them and their late owners is so strong as it was in the instances which have come under our notice.

Q. (By another Sitter.) But surely you do not mean to say that the countless billions and trillions of animals which have existed on earth since the day when the first signs of animal life appeared on earth, live on after their deaths? How could there possibly be space for them in the spheres?

A. Friend, I will answer your question as to what Space is, when you tell me what Eternity is.

The Spirit of the animal—more especially of the animal in which affection has been stimulated during its life on earth—clothed in its spiritual-body, an exact counterpart of its earth-body when at its state of greatest perfection, with its spiritual counterpart of the brain, the mind, passes into the sphere in which the animals dwell, there to lead happy and contented lives, without fear of torture by either human beings or by other animals, for their innate love of slaughter, and all need for such slaughter is, at "death," removed from them forever. There the naturalist may solve the many problems connected with animal life of all kinds which so puzzled him when on earth. There, as was said by one of your ancient writers, "The wolf and the lamb, the leopard and the kid, lie down together," for even Nature's fiendish cruelties cannot touch them in that sphere. There the poor creature which during its earth-life suffered indescribable tortures at the hand of man, finds perfect peace and rest; and there the faithful friend of former years, be it beast or bird, will most assuredly be found waiting to welcome its loving master or mistress with the utmost joy: for Love is king there!

Q. You referred to "Nature's fiendish cruelties" just now. I cannot conceive the Creator of the human infant, for instance, creating the leopard to mangle and destroy that infant.

A. You will yet learn that there were many Creators. This fact is referred to in your sacred writings, where the Gods say, "Let us make man in our image and after our likeness."

PARTIAL AND FULL-FORM MATERIALISATIONS

We find that it is generally admitted by the entities that in order to economize "the power" during our experiments, and with a view to preventing the system of the Sensitive being drained of too much vitality, full-form materializations are rare; the majority being partial materializations only.

These may be classified as :

(1) A forehead, eyes and nose only, with no powers of speech. (2) A complete face, but minus the back of the head, with no powers of speech. (3) The head and neck, with vocal organs

complete. (4) The head, with neck and shoulders, arms and hands, but nothing more. (This is one of the most common.) (5) The head and body complete down to the waist only. (6) The head, complete body, with legs and feet: the rarest of all.

On several occasions strangers, who had been admitted to some of our experimental meetings as guests of our members, abused the hospitality thus shown to them by "breaking conditions" when we were experimenting in a subdued light, and were unable to see what they were doing. Quite half a dozen of these men have afterwards confessed that when a materialized form was opposite to them, and within two or three feet of them, and at a distance of two to three yards from the Sensitive, they had extended their legs and feet, and had passed them across and over the spot where the form was to be seen, in order that they might feel the lower limbs of the entity. But in every instance they have reported that nothing whatever obstructed the motion of their legs and feet, greatly to their confusion and surprise: in other words, they had found that there was nothing whatever tangible in the way of lower limbs attached to the upper portion of the materialized body in front of them; proving conclusively that the materialization was only a partial one, and was not full-form.

At an experimental meeting held at Batter-sea Rise, London, S.W.—men only being present, and Sir William Crookes' Sensitive, Mrs. Corner, acting as Sensitive for us—the French girl had been standing in our midst for nearly half an hour answering questions asked by medical men and other scientists, who formed the half-circle of Sitters on that occasion—questions which, with two exceptions, are not suitable for publication here.

Q. (By Dr A. C.) From your appearance, and the firmness of your arms, hands, and bust, I assume that you are at this moment fully materialized. Please show us your lower limbs so as to convince us of this fact?

A. No, Doctor, I cannot do that now, but if you will give me time to return to" Florrie" (the Sensitive) for two minutes, I will get more power, and will then gladly do so.

She returned to the spot where the Sensitive was seated on her chair in a state of deep trance; and in less than two minutes she once again walked into our midst, and lifting up her white draperies, showed us her legs bared from the knees downwards. She then placed one of her little feet upon Dr A. C.'s knee, and permitted him to touch both her leg and foot, in order to prove to him and to us that she was fully materialized in every respect.

Q. (By Dr A. C.) How is it that you had no lower limbs three minutes ago, and were obliged to return to the Sensitive before you could obtain them?

A. Doctor, when we come to you people on earth in this way, our great desire is that we may be recognized first by our voices, then by our faces. That is the reason why so many of us materialize only the head, throat, arms, and hands, and the upper portion of our bodies. That is quite enough for you to identify us by, as a rule, and in doing this we are able to save "the power" for the use of other entities who may wish to materialize as soon as we have finished.

Tonight there is any amount of "power" here, as you seven men are all in such good health; and as only two of us intend to use it, I am able to show myself to you fully materialized from head to foot, just as my predecessor "Katie" used to do, through this very Sensitive, to Sir William Crookes. But you may take it from me as a fact that full-form materializations in this country are rare, for the reason which I have stated; the vast majority being partial materializations only.

LOOSENING THE TIES

Q. Will you explain more clearly what you mean by urging upon us to leave all undesirable earth-conditions behind us, when we pass out of our physical-bodies at the change which we term "death"?

A. Friend, could you but witness the pitiful sights which we see around us, as we carry on our mission work amongst the inhabitants of the First Sphere, you would realize the vast importance of our frequent injunction to you all to loosen your earth-ties before passing out of your bodies, so that such ties shall not tend to draw you back to earth in order that you may obtain a sense of gratification from them.

Had you developed your gift of clairvoyance (or clear seeing) there would be no need for you to ask such a question as this of us, as you would be able to see for yourself, with your spiritual sight, at any time if you chose to do so, the miseries endured by the unhappy beings from the First Sphere; the earthbound Spirits of men and women of all classes, from the very highest socially down to the very poorest and most degraded—earth-bound Spirits who crowd your cities, towns, and villages, day and night, seeking to gratify, yes, and actually gratifying, their animal natures (the ones which they have brought over to that sphere from your earth) through the instrumentality of the unhappy beings, the carnal-minded men and women of earth of all classes, who these First Sphere entities are able to control and use for this special purpose; so true it is, in both your world and ours, that "like attracts like."

Gambling, the love of dress, the love of your cruel blood-sports, and the love of gold, hold legions of well-educated, as well as ignorant, men and women, who have passed out of their bodies for the last time, closely to earth.

Gluttony, the inordinate desire for food, and even worse, insobriety, the craving for intoxicating drink; and yet one state even lower still, animalism, the craving for sensuality—these hold countless legions of all classes to earth as earth-bound Spirits, who seek to gratify, and do actually gratify, those desires, through the carnal-minded people who exist in such vast numbers on your earth today.

Round your banqueting halls, your restaurants and eating-houses, swarm legions of those from the First Sphere who still crave for the food of earth—the carnivorous man or woman, the gourmand, the glutton—endeavoring to gratify themselves, as Spirits, through the excesses of the human epicures they overshadow as they feast.

Round the drinking saloons of your hotels, round the bars of your inns and public-houses, swarm legions of those from the First Sphere, craving for alcoholic drink; and not only satisfying this craving as the wretched mortal imbibes his (or her) wine, beer, or alcohol, but actually urging that mortal to buy, or even to steal, more and more, until at length he (or she) falls to the ground helpless, as miserable drunkard; the controlling, overshadowing being from the

First Sphere reveling in their drunkenness, as it satisfies their craving for alcohol for a time.

And this is true also of animalism, sensuality: your public parks and open spaces, your brothels and "dens of infamy," as you term them, are surrounded day and night by countless legions of those from the First Sphere, who seek to gratify, and do actually gratify, their animal desires, through the actions of the men and women of earth, the carnal-minded ones, who are imbued with similar desires and are able to carry them into effect; the controlling, overshadowing beings from the First Sphere urging them on to greater and still greater excesses, until at length the unhappy mortal drifts into the hospitals specially prepared to receive such cases, into the prisons, the asylums, or even terminates his (or her) earth-life as a suicide, through his animalism.

Can you wonder, then, that knowing as we do of the horrors awaiting those who pass out of their earth-bodies with their animal passions still enthralling them in their deadly embrace, can you wonder that we urge upon you to "loosen the ties" of earth; to so master yourselves here and now that you shall leave behind you forever all undesirable conditions on earth, when you pass out of your physical bodies for the last time and enter upon "the spheres of active life"?

FRAUDULENT PHENOMENA

Q. (By G. B.) We find that one of the greatest obstacles in the way of inducing scientifically trained men and women to investigate the claims made by you entities that the phenomena which you offer for our investigation are genuine—is the fear that they may be cleverly tricked by the Sensitive or his confederates, and that an investigation under such conditions as these is therefore a mere waste of time. Can you help us to answer such objections?

A. Friend, you will find that fraud is to be found in practically everything on earth: sport, trade, professions, politics, art, science, and above all in every one of the numerous religions of earth without exception; but that undoubted fact does not prove that there is nothing genuine in any of them. And the ideal investigator, the happy possessor of an open, and, consequently, well-balanced mind, instead of passing an off-hand judgment—that as all of them are known to be stained deeply with fraud, they are not worthy of his consideration—will carefully sift out for himself the golden grains of wheat from the mass of useless chaff.

This is the spirit in which the investigator of the claims made by us—that the phenomena witnessed at your experimental meetings are perfectly genuine—should commence and should carry on his inquiry into these matters; matters of the most profound importance to him.

Now, in dealing with the general question of fraudulent practices in connection with the production of physical phenomena—which, of course, includes what you all so wrongly term "materializations"—let us say at once that we fully realize the possibility of this, and will deal with the matter under two heads, viz. :—Conscious fraud on the part of the Sensitive and his confederates.

Unconscious fraud on the part of the Sensitive; which really amounts to conscious fraud on the part of the controlling entity, operating through the unconscious Sensitive.

In a previous chapter you have dealt fully with the precautions which you, as an expert, consider should be taken in order to prevent conscious fraud. on the part of the Sensitive and his confederates; and with these precautions I fully agree. Train your Sensitives to sit always in the light; strong light, somewhat shaded, in order to counteract the effects of the vibrations given off by the actinic rays in the light, so that they shall not unduly interfere with our work during our experiments with you.

Train your Sensitives and your Sitters to submit cheerfully at all times, when they are called upon to do so, to a close search of their bodies and their clothing, in order to prove to investigators that they have nothing concealed about them which could by any possibility be used in the production of fraudulent phenomena.

Under conditions such as these—conditions which you imposed upon that fine Sensitive, Florrie Cook (Mrs. Corner), again and again during your experiments with her—conscious fraud on the part of any Sensitive or his confederates is, in my opinion, absolutely impossible.

We have now to deal with unconscious fraud on the part of the Sensitive, which really amounts to conscious fraud on the part of the entity controlling the unconscious Sensitive. Under this section of our subject I include the substitution, without due notice being given, of transfigurations for materializations, to which we have already referred.

As this substitution can only, as a rule, take place in darkness, the remedy is a simple one. Refuse to sit in darkness, unless the controlling entity (the leader) pledges his word not to produce transfigurations without your consent; and further, pledges himself to produce proof of this, if called upon to do so, at any time during the experiment.

We say this as much on behalf of the Sensitive himself as on behalf of the experimenters: for should the conditions be broken at any moment when the transfigured Sensitive, brought from his chair in a state of complete insensibility by the controlling entity, is in their midst, and is seized by any of the Sitters, the result invariably is of course that, on turning up the lights, the unfortunate Sensitive himself is found to be struggling violently in the hands of his captors, who at once proceed to denounce him as a cheat and a fraud, and prosecute him in a court of law.

The officials of your society must deal sternly with any entity who produces a transfiguration during your experiments, without giving due warning to all present that he intends to do so; and should this occur a second time, you would be fully justified in refusing to take part in any experimental meeting at which the offending entity was permitted to operate as leader. I say this advisedly, and quite as much for the sake of the innocent Sensitive as for the sake of the experimenters. Equally sternly should the officials of your society deal with any entity who passes from outside objects into the room where your experiments are being conducted, without giving notice to all present that he intends to do so, as great harm is done to the reputation of the unconscious and entirely innocent Sensitive by such ill-advised action, if for any reason the entity finds himself unable to remove the object from the room before the close of the experiment.

Let me explain this more fully by means of a simple illustration.

The Sensitive is sitting in his chair in a state of deep trance, and a materialized entity is about to leave the spot, close to the Sensitive, where it has built up the body which it desires to show to the Sitters; but finding that, for the purpose of identification, the entity inhabiting the temporary body should bring with him—shall we say—a peculiarly shaped walking-stick which he always used when living on earth, a pause is made, whilst one of the entities assisting at the experiment makes diligent search in the neighborhood for a stick of that particular pattern.

Happening to find one in a house, say half a mile away, he quickly passes it through space—through what you term solid matter, such as walls, roof, and ceiling—and hands it to the waiting entity, who walks out amongst the Sitters carrying it, or leaning upon it, in exactly the same way in which he did when he lived on earth.

The entity, greatly to his joy, is recognized at once, the presence of the peculiarly shaped walking-stick making the proof of his identity doubly sure. And there the matter would end in the ordinary way; for as soon as the controlling entity had returned to our sphere, one of the others would take the stick back to the exact spot from whence he had brought it for temporary use during the experiment.

But let the conditions be broken: imagine that the materialized entity is suddenly seized by one of the Sitters before it can return to the unconscious Sensitive, and there on the floor lies the solid walking-stick!

Try as the captor will, he cannot hold the materialized form in his arms, for it will at once commence to fade away, however tightly he may clasp it, and will pass swiftly back to the Sensitive.

The clothing, the drapery, in which the figure was temporarily clad, will also be found to have faded away, without leaving the slightest trace of its presence; but there on the floor lies the solid walking-stick, a truly damning piece of evidence against the unfortunate Sensitive; for try as he will, the entity who ordered the stick to be brought into the room is altogether unable to get it back to the place from whence he had obtained it, owing to the disturbed conditions caused by the attempted capture of the materialized form: and although its appearance on the floor is in itself a marvelous proof to the experimenters of what can be done by an entity who understands the laws of passing "matter through matter," as you term it, the investigator, who knows nothing whatever concerning these laws, who probably has never witnessed the apparent penetration of matter by matter before—although freely admitting the impossibility of the stick having been hidden in the empty room before the experiment began—at once jumps to the conclusion that the walking-stick lying on the floor before him is proof positive that he has been tricked in some way by the Sensitive, and that he is nothing but a swindler and a fraud.

He then proceeds to "expose" him, in the public press and elsewhere; and in doing so, merely exposes his own crass ignorance of the laws which govern the production of physical phenomena of all kinds, and becomes the laughing-stock of those experimenters who have progressed sufficiently in their investigations to be able to grasp the fact that such laws do actually exist, and are immutable.

Before condemning any Sensitive as an impostor we would urge upon you first to make careful inquiry as to who is really to blame; and in many instances you will be surprised to find that—as in my little illustration—the offender is one from our dimension, and that the entirely innocent Sensitive has been made the victim of certain circumstances over which he had no control whatever, the real offender, the controlling entity, escaping scot-free.

In conclusion, we would ask you to remember always that the phenomena which we are permitted to produce for you, highly important as they undoubtedly are, must be used for one purpose and one purpose only—the higher, purer development of yourselves whilst here on earth, your own spiritual development: that they are but the alpha only, not the omega, merely the beginning for the investigator, not the end.

We come to you beings of earth to do something more than merely to prove our existence in another sphere, and to present wonders to marvel-seekers. We mean serious and practical work for human enlightenment and progress. We come to teach a truer, brighter, and better philosophy of life than the world has yet had: to aid you in the solution of the great problems of your being: to inspire you with higher aims and nobler efforts for your own and for others' good: to give you the benefit of our larger experience that you may be incited to make the most and best of your earthly opportunities: and to do what we can to correct your errors, and to educate you for the practical duties of both the present and the future life.

In fact, our purposes for your good are manifold beyond the demonstrations of our presence; and those investigators who stop short with phenomenal manifestations, and do not make them stepping-stones leading upwards to the great temple of Spiritual Truth, are but idle spectators of a "dumb show" that may amaze and perhaps amuse them for a time, without adding anything to their mental or spiritual growth.

After receiving tests enough to convince a reasonable mind of the reality of Spirit intercourse, the clamor for "a sign" should cease; and where it continues month after month, and year after year, as is lamentably the case with many, it evinces a morbid condition of mind; and the constant attendance at experimental meetings to obtain a sensuous phenomena becomes a mental dissipation, ending in fanaticism, and a waste of time, money, and vital force, if nothing worse.

APPENDIX

During the four years 1909—1913, a series of carefully conducted experiments were carried out under very strict test conditions in France and Germany, by a number of scientists headed by Baron von Schrenck-Notzing of Munich, a medical man, described as one of the greatest of German authorities on this subject, in an endeavor to solve various problems connected with the existence of the plastic substance, which he has named "teleplasma."

The results of their investigations have now been published by the Baron in a large volume (freely illustrated with photographs and sketches) entitled Materializations Phaenomene, the photographs showing clearly both the vapour-like and the dough-like substances in the "atmoplastic" and" pachyplastic" stages of the evolution of the complete "teleplasma."

This is seen to be issuing from different portions of the bodies of the Sensitive B, and actually passing through the fine meshes of the muslin in which their bodies were frequently enveloped; the Sensitives' hands, and sometimes their feet as well, being held firmly by the experimenters.

And more than this, they obtained on two occasions portions of the "teleplasma," which were submitted to analytical and microscopic examinations. The results are appended.

The Sensitives were two young women, Mlle. Marthe Berand, aged 23, and Mlle. Stanislawa P., aged 19, both of them, in the cause of science, voluntarily and without payment of any kind, submitting themselves to the most searching examinations and most stringent tests, sitting (always in red light) even entirely nude during many of the experiments, and freely permitting the medical men present to examine every portion of their naked bodies at any moment.

The two hundred photographs (including a cinematograph record) were taken by flash-light: and on one occasion no less than nine photographic cameras, set at various angles, were exposed on Mlle. Marthe simultaneously.

In order to avoid the constant repetition of names, I will refer to the three experimenters from whose reports I have quoted, as A (the leader), B, and C (a scientific sceptic of note).

Those who have investigated the phenomena termed "materializations" closely, are well aware of the fact that before an entity can appear in either a partially or fully formed (temporary) body, it must procure from the Sensitive and the Sitters material to be used in four different ways, viz. :

(1) The formation of the solid portions, such as bones, skull, teeth, nails, etc.;

(2) The formation of the soft portions, such as the flesh, the heart, lungs, intestines, etc., and an outer skin, colored either white, yellow, brown, or black, according to the (alleged) nationality of the controlling entity during its earth-life;

(3) The formation of the hair on the body, either dark, fair, or grey;

(4) The formation of clothing of various materials and colors; and on reading the abbreviated reports, it will be noticed how greatly the descriptions vary, just as one would anticipate, seeing that the "teleplasma" was handled indiscriminately by A, B, and C during the atmoplastic and pachyplastic stages of its evolution.

A, on handling the "pachyplasma," reports that his fingers touched "a firm, dark (nearly black-looking) substance, comparable to touching the dark skin of a mushroom." Again: "A firm, cool, damp substance, which vanished on touch." Again: "A damp, cold, band-like webbing." Again: "Its touch gave the impression of an organic damp substance."

He is permitted to place his hand in "atmoplasma" issuing from the Sensitive, and says," I had the impression of destroying as it were a spider's web." (Possibly a portion of (4) forming into clothing.—(G. B.)

B observes a kind of veil proceeding from the Sensitive's neck; it hangs over her arm, and descends to the floor. B's hand is led by the left hand of the Sensitive (which B is holding firmly, A holding her right hand) towards the veiling, and grasps it. (Possibly a portion of (4) clothing fully developed.—(G. B.)

Later B reports: "I suddenly felt a cool, sticky mass touching my hand. I held it firmly and drew it carefully towards me, without releasing the right hand of the Sensitive; C holding her left hand. The mass elongated itself in my fingers, hung down from my hand, and I was able to observe it for one or two minutes. . . . As I continued to draw the matter carefully asunder, it disappeared from my hand." B describes it as "a flat, streaky, thread-like, sticky, cool, living substance, without smell; of light grey-whitish color. My fingers remained damp from the contact." B followed the mass held in the hand right up to its source from the left shoulder of the Sensitive, describing it as "a crude knot of dense, tough substance." Again: "Damp, cold, sticky, and gave the impression of a fibrous, irregularly formed long strip of skin of definite consistency and shape." ("Cold and clammy and without smell," was my impression.—(G. B.). P.28.)

B picks off a small portion of the sticky mass, and on pulling it apart finds that only hair is left in the hand; hair of a totally different shade to that of the Sensitive. (Possibly a portion of (3) hair information.—(G. B)

B sees the substance issuing in large quantities from the mouth of the Sensitive. A portion lay on A's hand for six seconds and was photographed by B. "It appeared to be partly transparent and of rubber-like elasticity. In proportion to its bulk, it felt heavy: a heavy organic substance comparable to membranous (intestinal) matter." (Possibly a portion of (2) forming into intestines.—(G. B.)

B touches some of the substance lying on the lap of the Sensitive, and finds "a firm, hard, rounded article with rough upper surface: it felt something like a bone." (Possibly a portion of (1) bone formation .—(G. B.)

C describes the substance as "cool, comparatively heavy in weight, with a feeling as if a small reptile had rested in my hand." Again: "Reptile-like, damp, cold skin."

The photographs show plainly atmoplasma, the" vapor-like substance," forming round the head of the Sensitive like a cloud; and also pachyplasma, the "dough-like substance," issuing in (1) narrow or wide bands (strips); (2) large masses; (3) cords, resembling the human umbilicus closely: like coarse or fine string, and like thread.

It is shown issuing (in masses) from the top, sides, and back of the head of the Sensitive, at times completely enveloping the head; from the mouth (in bands and in streams) and neck; from both shoulders (in large masses); ex mammis, ex umbilico et vagina: generally working its way downwards by force of gravity, but frequently issuing en vagina et umbilico and working its way upwards with reptile-like motion to the mouth, or suspending itself gracefully de mammis. (Showing signs of intelligence in the designs, and moving apparently of its own volition.—(G. B.)

The Sensitive places one foot across the knees of A, and the other across the knees of C, each of them holding one of her hands, and pachyplasma is shown issuing in masses en umbilico et vagina.

It seems probable that the portions of the body in which the substance is formed are the great nerve-centers, the solar plexus, the pineal gland, the brain, and spine; and that it then exudes from the orifices in the body nearest to those nerve-centers, viz, the mouth, the ears, mammae, umbilicus, and in the case of female Sensitives, en vagina. —(G. B.)

With the idea of obtaining a portion of the substance which he could submit to a microscopical and analytical examination, A provided himself with a small metal box, lined with porcelain, and having a tightly fitting lid; and this box he kept carefully in his pocket at all times, in case it should be suddenly required.

Both A and B succeeded in obtaining portions of "teleplasma": the report given by A stating that (while the Sensitive's hands were clearly visible) he held the box open about twelve inches above her right hand. "Three fingers formed, which first touched the box, then dipped into it, and made several shaking movements. I clapped the cover on, and put the box in my pocket."

On another occasion (when the Sensitive's hands were securely held by A and B) B holds the box, and "a long, skin-like strip of the substance glides with creepy movement from the mouth of the Sensitive over her left forearm, and deposits a small fragment of the substance in the box. Quick as lightning the remainder of the substance flies back to the Sensitive. This is repeated again and again, and by the fifth attempt the substance fills the box, doing so by falling in spirals by force of gravity."

The portion obtained by A, when examined by electric light, was seen to consist of two small particles of matter, one piece measuring 0.63 inch long, by 0.43 inch wide, with a thickness of 0.09 inch: the thinner and finer portion being 0.47 inch in diameter. When examined they were recognized as portions of human skin. A microphotograph of this is given. (Possibly pieces of (2) skin formation.—(G. B.)) Under microscopical examination pigmental epithelial cells were clearly shown. The Sensitive was at once examined, but no particle of her skin was found to be missing.

The portion obtained by B, on examination by electric light, was found to consist of about a quarter of a cubic pint of a transparent slimy fluid without air bubbles.

(Had the box been warmed to blood heat, the substance might not have liquefied so quickly. The contact with the cold enamel should have been avoided.—(G. B.))

ANALYSIS.—Colorless. slightly cloudy, fluid (not thready), no smell: traces of cell detritus and sputum (spittle). Deposit, whitish. Reaction, slightly alkaline.

MICROSCOPIC EXAMINATION.—Numerous skin discs: some sputum-like bodies: numerous granulates of the mucous membrane: numerous minute particles of flesh: traces of "sulphozyansaurem" potash. The dried residues weighed 860 gr. per liter. Three gr. of ash.

Attention is called to the fact that the substance under examination, having passed through the mouth of the Sensitive, it is but natural that traces of sputum and minute fragments of the food last eaten by her should be revealed by the examination.

The author (A) admits that the existence of the substance in both the vapor-like and the dough-like (autoplastic and pachyplastic) stages of its evolution is proved; and describes the teleplasma as "a kind of transitory matter arising in an unknown manner, possessing biological functions and powers of transformation, depending in a very special degree upon the psychic influence of the person tested."

www.ingramcontent.com/pod-product-compliance
Lightning Source LLC
LaVergne TN
LVHW041633070426
835507LV00008B/603